THE DREAM

The Story of the 1978 and 1979 Peerless Panthers

THE DREAM

The Story of the 1978 and 1979 Peerless Panthers

Joe Puckett

Aubade Publishing
Amherst, NH

Library of Congress Control Number: 2010906390

ISBN: 978-0-9845494-0-5

Published by Aubade Publishing Amherst, NH

Printed in the United States of America

For Vonda, Cosette and Emma

Contents

Foreword

This story, I have to warn you up front, is unabashedly and shamelessly nostalgic—recalling a time and place in my life when my goal each morning when I woke up was to play as much as possible before the sun went down and get up the next morning to do exactly the same thing. Although the key events in the narrative happened over 30 years ago now, my memories of most of the events in the story are still fairly vivid, owing largely to the fact that, quite frankly, there was not a lot else occupying my mind at the time.

Life for me growing up in the 1960's and 70's in the small farming and ranching community of Peerless, Montana was very simple. Eat, sleep, play all day, and go to church on Sunday—that was about it. About the only thing that changed in this cycle was what game I played, which depended on what time of year it was. But the particular sport I played that this story revolves around is basketball—a game for which I still have a tremendous passion and love.

As you shall read in the following pages, the closure of Peerless High School (PHS) in June 2009 is what prompted me to write this story. I wanted to keep the memory of PHS and the memory of the Peerless community alive. And, although I can never feel anything but sadness when I think about Peerless High School closing, I suppose I can take some consolation in the fact that if it hadn't, I may have never written this story, which for me has been an incredibly enjoyable and rewarding experience. I can only hope you enjoy reading it half as much as I've enjoyed writing it.

Joe Puckett, May 1, 2010

Acknowledgements

I would like to thank Wallace Fladager for starting the "Peerless People" discussion group on Facebook, Mike Anderson for sending me the email about the group, Warren Fladager for encouraging me to write, Kathleen Fladager for asking me to write about the 1978 and 1979 Peerless Panthers, Brian Bechtold for his encouragement to publish this story, and Hank Burgess and Emily Stueven for their superb editing. I would also like to thank all of my teammates at Peerless through the years (especially my brother Jon), Superintendent Marvin Hash, my outstanding high school coaches, Ron Scott, Rollin Rieger, Clark Shaffer, Brian Bechtold, "Diamond" Jim Niccum, , and the entire Peerless community. And finally, I'd like to thank the greatest motivator I've ever known in my life, Kelvin Sampson, my coach at Montana Tech from 1981–1984.

Dedication

This book is dedicated to my mom and dad, Faustine and George "Tiny" Puckett, who did everything they possibly could to help their two boys realize their dream, and to all parents, who when they recognize a dream in a child, do everything in their power to ensure they have every opportunity to fulfill it.

Prologue

A True Story

This is a true story. It is basically a story about two brothers and their dad, who, together with their childhood basketball teammates, shared a lifelong dream to someday play in and win the State Class C basketball tournament in Helena, Montana for the first time in the school's history. The time for the climax of the story is the years 1978 and 1979, and the place is a small town in the extreme northeastern part of the state of Montana, a town called Peerless. The years 1978 and 1979 were my junior and senior years at Peerless High School, a school that no longer exists.

The End of an Era

This story is also the story about the ending of an era, a passing of a way of life for many people that live on the highline in northeastern Montana. It is the story of a passing of what was once the most powerful Class C conference in the entire state of Montana, District 1-C, consisting at the time of the high schools of Peerless, Outlook, Flaxville, Westby, Antelope and Medicine Lake, who during a six year span, 1975–80, won five out of six State C basketball championships. Medicine Lake won the State Class B championship in 1975. Westby won the State championship in 1972. Between the years 1970–1980, District 1-C won the Eastern Divisional tournament nine out of eleven times. During this time the District was the most dominant in the entire history of Montana Class C basketball, as in two of those years, a team from District 1-C also finished second at State, losing only to the champion from 1-C. That was

Antelope losing to Westby in 1975 and Peerless losing to Flaxville in 1979. Also, in 1980, the last year the State tournament was played in Helena, Outlook and Opheim (a former 1-C team) finished 1–2 at State. Four of these high schools, Peerless, Outlook, Flaxville and Antelope, no longer exist, and this story is being told so that people can remember that some of the finest Class C basketball ever played in the state of Montana came from these small schools in this District.

Basketball Mecca

The story is also the story about a passing of a time when the State Class C basketball tournament was held every year in Helena. For 24 consecutive years, between the years 1957–1980, the State Class C basketball tournament in Montana was held in the state capital, Helena. Beginning in 1975, my dad would take my brother Jon and me and some of our teammates to watch the State tournament in Helena, at the Carroll College Physical Education Center; this was always the most exciting trip for me of the entire year. Prior to 1975, I would listen to the State tournament games on the radio and follow the results in the newspaper. It was always my dream to make it to Helena someday as a player and play on that court, a court where I had watched so many exciting State tournament games, and saw so many champions crowned.

PHS Passes

This is also the story about the passing of Peerless High School (PHS) and the Peerless Panthers basketball team, with the tremendous passion, dedication and absolute love for the game of basketball that its players possessed. Peerless High School was founded by my grandfather, Forgey Reese Puckett, in 1932. My grandpa originally came from Tennessee. Born there in 1886, he moved to Montana to teach in 1916. He was the principal at Ryegate for four years (where my dad was born), then in the small Montana towns of Victor, Antelope, Dooley, Cardwell (near Whitehall) and finally Peerless in

Forgey Reese Puckett, Principal of PHS, 1932–1942, with his three sons (from left) Ed, George "Tiny", and Reese.

1932, where he was principal until he died in1942.

While he was at Peerless, he instituted the concept of a non-profit dormitory whereby many farm children could take advantage of a high school education at a minimum of expense to their parents. In 1934 and 1935, he arranged for two additions to the school building which were used as boys and girls dormitories where the students could furnish their own meat, vegetables and other food produce paying only about $6 a month for their room and board. This practice, which was still going on at the time of his death in 1942, enabled many students to attend school who otherwise could not afford to.

My grandpa came from a large farm in Tennessee. One day, curious boy that I was, I asked Dad why my grandpa left the farm in Tennessee to become a teacher and move to Montana. My dad told me—and I can't sugarcoat this because this is exactly how Dad would say what my grandpa said—"I got sick and tired of lookin' that ol' mule up the ass!"

Peerless Schools closed in Jun 2009, due to lack of student population. Through the years, the decline in the ability of the small farmer and rancher to make a living gradually reduced the enrollment to the point that the school could no longer operate on its own. My Uncle Reese graduated in 1933 and Uncle Ed was in the graduating class of 1934. My dad graduated in 1937 and my mom graduated in 1939. My cousin Terry Puckett, was the last superintendent of the school, in 2008–09. This story is being told to keep the memory of Peerless High School alive, and to help people remember that this small town, and this small school, once played some of the most inspired basketball in the history of Class C.

The Dream

But most of all, this is a story about a dream, a dream that a group of boys shared to someday play in the State Class C tournament in Montana, then to win the State championship game for their small school. So this is a story about dreams, rivalries, triumph, disappointment, passion, and a love that was shared by a group of boys who never gave up striving for the one thing in their life that mattered most to them: Playing in the State Class C basketball tournament in Montana.

How It Came to Be

So what prompted me to write about this experience? In the spring of 2009, I received an email from Mike Anderson (PHS '95), a fellow Peerless graduate whom I didn't even know at the time, and still haven't met. His email provided me with a link to a discussion group called "Peerless People" on Facebook. He suggested I check it out and perhaps share some stories about my experiences growing up in Peerless with the rest of the group. So I decided to check it out. I began to read some of the wonderful stories that were being written by people like Warren Fladager (PHS '69) and Wallace Fladager (PHS '71), amazing storytellers who wrote about earlier (1950's and 60's) Peerless experiences and the old buildings in the town, interesting characters who lived in the town, stuff like that. After reading some of these enjoyable stories myself, I began to write a few of my own, with topics like "Winter Memories" and the "Old School and Other Missing Buildings."

Then one day something caught my eye: On the top of the discussion group page I read the words, "Peerless School closes its doors in Jun 2009." This shocked me: I knew the school was in an enrollment decline, but I had lived away from Peerless for so long I wasn't aware of just how desperate the situation had become. Then I realized that the purpose of the Facebook discussion group was to tell the stories about growing up in Peerless so that the town and the school would not be forgotten. Suddenly writing the stories took on new meaning for me.

Shortly after I discovered that the school was closing, Kathleen Fladager (PHS '76) began a new discussion topic simply titled "Basketball." She started it off by writing about the "Greatest Shot in Peerless Basketball History," by Steve Miner (PHS '75), which I remember well because it happened in 1974, when I was a seventh grader. So I began to write some little stories about basketball in this topic, a topic I knew a little bit about! Then Kathleen asked to write about the first ever trip to State tournament by a Peerless Panther team, the 1978 Panthers. I began writing the story of the 1978 Panthers, about how the 1978 Peerless team became the first team in the 45-year history of the school to make it to State. Then, I followed up with the story of the 1979 Panthers, my senior year, a team that won the first Conference and District championships for Peerless, and came within an arms grasp of attaining our ultimate goal, that of winning the State Class C basketball championship.

The Seeds
of the Dream

A Simple Life

For me, growing up in the small town of Peerless, Montana in the 1960's and 1970's was a very simple life. There weren't many distractions, or a lot of opportunities to get in trouble, although I managed to do that occasionally! In our house, we had a TV with an antenna, and, depending on the cloud cover on any particular day, we were able to receive three TV channels, two of which were Canadian. In fact, by way of sports viewing, I watched more ice hockey while growing up than any other sport. Every Wednesday night was "Hockey Night in Canada." I loved to watch these games. This was when they actually skated and played hockey, before it became boxing and wrestling on skates. But that's another story . . .

Altar of St. Ann's
Church, Peerless.

We did not have a VCR to play movies or video games. To pass the time, my twin brother Jon and I spent most of our time playing basketball and baseball, which our dad, George "Tiny" Puckett, coached us in up until we were fifth graders in basketball, and eighth graders in baseball. Our favorite sport, by far, was basketball.

I was raised Roman Catholic, and regularly attended church on Sunday with my family. I loved the structure, repetition and rhythm of the Catholic Church, as I loved the structure, repetition and rhythm of my simple life. Interestingly, the years for me were not marked by harvest in fall, the falling (and blowing!) snow in winter, the sound of the first meadowlark in spring, or the heat of the summer sun, but by the changing seasons of sports. My "New Year" really began a little before school started in August, when I, along with my brother Jon, would begin training for cross country. At this time, we would also begin to play basketball in the gym every night, just as the rest of the kids in the small farming and ranching community of Peerless would begin to let summer go after harvest and begin to look forward to school as well. cross country ended the last days of October. Basketball practice would begin the first week in November. We would play our first basketball game of the season the day after Thanksgiving, then in a Christmas tournament right before Christmas. In early February, the basketball tournaments started, which ran through the first part of March, my birthday. Then it was track and field in the spring, and onto baseball in the summer. Once summer began winding down in August, the new cross country season would begin the sporting cycle anew. Now that I look back on it, I lived a very closed and sheltered life. Now this wasn't intentional; it was merely a function of the time and place in which I lived, and I was very, very happy living this life.

The Only Game in Town

Since Peerless was a small school, with an enrollment maybe averaging between 25–30 students in grades nine through twelve, basketball was the only game in town. We didn't have a high school football or baseball team. The primary social event, especially in the winter, was a basketball game on Friday or Saturday night. The entire community would congregate at the Peerless Gym to cheer on the Peerless Panthers on those cold winter nights in northeastern Montana, then travel with the team to nearby towns to watch us play there as well. After the games, most of the people would make the short trip from the gym to the Peerless Bar, to have a beer (or two) and discuss the game.

How to Make It to State

Of the four classifications for basketball in Montana, Class C is the smallest, but even by Class C standards, Peerless was a small school. There are about 95 schools in Class C in Montana, organized into thirteen Districts and four Divisions. The District I played in was District 1-C, which no longer exists. When I played, there were six teams in the District, although at one time there were eight. Beginning in February of each year, following the regular season, Class C schools would compete in three tournaments to determine the State Class C champion; namely, District, Divisional, and State. At the time, in order to advance to Divisional, a team had to place either first, second or third at District tournament, but every third year you had to place at least second at District. This was because there were three Districts represented at the Eastern Divisional (1-C, 2-C and 3-C). So each year two Districts would send three teams, but one District could only send two, because the Divisional tournament was composed of eight teams. After qualifying for Divisional, a team had to finish either first or second to advance to the State tournament. Many times at Divisional (and sometimes at District), there would be a challenge game between the third place team at the tournament and the second place team, if they had not previously met each other in that tournament. The winner of that game, always played on a Monday night, would advance to the next tournament.

Through the years, Peerless was not very successful in high school basketball; however, in 1937, my dad's team took third place at District, winning the consolation. But back then the tournament was single elimination, so his team did not advance. Up until 1974, (41 years after the school was founded), the third place at District in 1937 was the best Peerless had ever done, so we had never qualified for Divisional tournament. Up until 1978, my junior year in high school, Peerless had never in its 45-year history made it to the State tournament, and in fact had never even played for the *chance* to go. But 1978 would change everything, and the lifelong dream that my dad, my brother Jon and me, and all our teammates shared came true, in a very remarkable and magical way.

Peerless Panthers, 1937 District 1 Consolation winners.

The Pirates of the Prairie

My passion for basketball was passed down to me from my father, as he simply *loved* the game of basketball. He played at Peerless High School, and after that he played for the Peerless Pirates, an independent town team that he played on with his brothers, Reese and Ed, the Halvorson brothers, Indy, Ernie and Ric, Alfie Dighans and many, many other players from the late 1930's through the 1950's. In fact, an entire book itself could be written about the Pirates; they were legendary in northeastern Montana. Since I was not born until 1961, Dad's years with the Pirates were over, so I never actually got to see him play in his prime, but Warren Fladager, fellow PHS graduate and a great storyteller, passes this oral tradition onto us about the Peerless Pirates on the Peerless People discussion group on Facebook:

Since I was not born until 1951, all I know is stories and conversations I heard and listened to from relatives and older people who lived it, as well as from old photos of those times.

A set shot was all anyone ever really shot (quite easily defended) so scores were very low.

Tiny Puckett developed a shot on the run off the dribble. I saw him shoot that shot in practice when we were very young! Well with that shot that no one expected him to shoot, he could score at will. He could break off a screen and shoot on the run, rather than stop, set his feet, and shoot a set shot. It was undefendable at the time, because people didn't expect it.

Scores were high from Peerless teams with that one shot, and along the way Reese Puckett perfected the inside game with new moves. Reese learned to play with his back to the basket where he developed the 'Turn around Jump Shot' under the basket, and he taught it to any player that would listen, me included.

Basically Tiny would either shoot or throw in to Reese, the center. Reese would head fake one way, turn and jump shoot the other way before he could get surrounded by everyone. Actually he developed the 'Jump Shot.' Most everyone shot flat footed before that.

These are all moves everyone knows now, but at that time almost no one did around the farming communities 'Town Team's' (and there were no coaches who could teach it.) The pro's knew most of these moves, but 'Town Team Basketball' was more like football in the early days. From 1910 thru the 20's, it was played with wire around the outside of the court, and fouls were rarely called, (the word "Cagers" for basketball players) came from those days.

The Puckett brothers brought the game into modern basketball, but they were not alone in the development of 'The Peerless Pirates' basketball early days.

Big 6' 6" Alf (Alfred) Dighans was an unstoppable center; I think John Dighans had a run with them as well. There were three Halvorson brothers (Indy, Ernie and Ric). My Uncle Lloyd Fladager 6' 1" (a natural athlete), and maybe a Larson or two. There were many others that played with the Pirates in the early days. All those I named were of German or Norwegian origin (an interesting side point!!)

But the core group were the three Puckett brothers (Reese, Ed, Tiny), the three Halvorson brothers (Indy, Ernie and Ric), and Alf Dighans. They had more fire power inside and out than most independent teams in the state. Gone were the days of low point games!! Tiny alone could outscore a team, with Reese

Peerless Pirates, 1939.

and Alfie inside scoring at will. Ed would camp out around the perimeter and when he got a pass he would 'catch and shoot' (also a new style of offense, no dribbling, just 'catch and shoot') The Halvorson brothers were strong, quick players. The team really didn't have any weaknesses. They won cash tournaments all across the states of Montana and North Dakota.

And they played professional traveling teams. The Pro's couldn't do their usual 'Fooling Around with the local team bit', they had to play hard! Peerless would regularly beat them.

I was just a kid when people would talk about those teams, and as I grew up , I ran into old players (opponents) that would tell me about playing against those teams. They would always mention how rough basketball was back then, as well as how good of shots the Pirates all were. Then they would chuckle (each one who told a story) and say, "And they always seemed like such nice guys!! UNTIL you started playing against them, then no more mister 'Nice Guy.' You had to go to work just to stay up with them!!"

One of the tournaments the Pirates played in that Warren Fladager refers to in the previous section was the Western Invitational

Tournament (WIT) in Lewistown, where the Pirates played in the early 1950's. Reese and Tiny made the all-WIT team. One of the "traveling Pros" Warren mentions that played against the Pirates was Marcus Haynes of the Harlem Globetrotters. He was elected to the pro basketball hall of fame in 1998, on the same ballot as Larry Bird. It is said that he considered "a guy with a tilted head from northeastern Montana" (that would be my Uncle Reese Puckett) to be one of the best ballplayers he ever played against.

Hoops in the Sahara

Dad's playing time with the Pirates was interrupted by his tour of duty with the Army Air Corps in World War II, from 1941–1945. But actually, World War II did not really stop my dad from playing basketball at all, as he figured out a way to continue to play just the same! It was in 1943 when he deployed with the 526th Fighter-Bomber Squadron of the 86th Fighter-Bomber Group to North Africa. The soldiers were allowed one standard issue suitcase to pack their stuff in, but they were not allowed to pack anything "non-essential." Apparently my dad considered a basketball rim, net, six deflated basketballs and an air pump to be "essential!" What he did was make a false bottom in the suitcase. He put some nails three inches above the bottom around the suitcase, put the rim, nets and deflated basketballs and pump in, then put a piece of wood that looked like the bottom of the suitcase over the nails. It worked! A portable basketball gym was transported to North Africa by the Army with all of his other "essential stuff". When he got to North Africa, he took out all his hidden contraband, put the net on the rim, inflated the basketballs and attached the rim to a large pole where they were quartered. He was shooting basketball in the Sahara Desert! His commanding officer looked at him, smiled and said, "Puck, only you could figure out a way to play basketball in Africa during this war!" My dad's nickname with his mates in World War II was "Puck", but he was always known as "Tiny" in the Peerless community.

Also, this story about my dad illustrates how he would always find a way to get around any obstacle, even if he had to bend the rules a little!

Early Hoop Memories

My first memory of playing basketball was in second grade, in the wintertime, when the weather would be so cold outside that we couldn't go out for recess at school. Our second grade teacher, Mrs. Saubak, would allow us to move the desks to one side of the room, and put a wastebasket up against the wall at the front of the classroom. Then, we would use a rubber ball, a kick ball, to play basketball. We would bounce the ball, pass to each other, defend, rebound, everything–just just as if this were a regular basketball game, except we would shoot the ball into the wastebasket. The girls in our class would be the cheerleaders, so they started to cheer in second grade as well. About the only thing we didn't have at that time was a band!

But even before my first memory of basketball in school, my dad claims we started playing basketball in our own living room at home. At the State tournament in 1978, he was interviewed by Dennis Gaub of the Billings Gazette. Dad was quoted as saying about his boys, "They were pretty lively. We had a pretty good-sized living room so I put up baskets at each end. I told my wife we'd buy new furniture later." I'm not sure how that comment was received by my mom, as she did not participate in the interview! Actually, my mom was always patient with the three of us and our sports obsession. She was always supportive, willing to take the back seat to let us have our fun through all those years.

The Young Team Forms

Competitive basketball in Peerless began in third grade. One of the things that was so special about playing Class C basketball in Montana while growing up is that you would have played basketball with the same group of boys from third grade through senior year in high school, a time span of ten years. Very early on, the group of boys I played with felt like we would be the team that would finally break through and be the first team from Peerless to make it to the State tournament.

In the wintertime, beginning in second grade, I would walk over to the old gym after school was over and watch the high school team's basketball practice. I can remember watching Gary Nieskens, Wallace Fladager, Terry Puckett, and other Peerless Panthers practice. Gene Thompson was their coach. Before practice started, when the players were shooting around, Jon and I would grab a ball and shoot baskets until the coach blew the whistle and practice started. After that, Jon and I would keep our ball and sit on the edge of the stage watching practice, waiting until the practice moved into a situation where the team was playing in the half court. Then, we would take our shoes off so we'd be quiet, tip-toe to the open side of the court and try to sneak a few shots. But Coach Thompson would get livid if the ball hit the floor when he was talking, so we had to be careful! What we had to learn to do, which in a funny way taught us to follow our shots, was to shoot, then run under the basket to catch the ball as it came through the net before it hit the floor! You couldn't shoot from too far out to do this, and *you couldn't miss!* After practice was over, we would again get to shoot around with the players after they ran line drills and shot free throws. When the players were showering, we could shoot by ourselves!

After that, we would go home, have dinner, and then come back up with Dad to play for another two hours. Dad would coach us, teach us the fundamentals. When I came up to the old gym with Dad at night, I remember when he would open the gym door and turn on the light to the entry way, there was enough light that would spill onto the court so I would run onto the court, find a basketball in the dark, and begin shooting with my coat and overshoes on. It took awhile for my eyes to adjust to the dark but I could actually see enough of the rim to get some decent shots off. I would do the same thing at the end of the night. Dad would turn the lights off to the gym, I would have my coat and overshoes on and would shoot until he got to the entry way and we finally had to go home. This was how Jon and I spent our winters in Peerless growing up.

In the winter, my favorite thing to do on Saturday mornings was

Basket in the backyard of the Puckett house in the wintertime.

to take out the trash because I would stop and shoot at the basket we had in the backyard. It didn't matter how much snow was there, I would have to make five shots before I went back in the house, no matter how cold it was. It was such a great feeling shooting out there on Saturday mornings, because we usually had a game later that day Saturday. I would imagine that I was playing in that game, that time was winding down, and it was me who was going to take the last shot. It was just the best feeling in the world the day of a game! One Friday night following a game, Jon was sleeping and woke up in the middle of the night with a terrible nightmare. He woke up everyone in the house. Mom came running in to ask what was wrong. Jon just asked Mom, "What day is it?". Mom said "It's Friday night." And then Jon just let out a huge sigh of relief and said, "Oh, I had a dream it was Saturday night and we didn't have another game this weekend!" He was very upset at that horrible thought of not another game that weekend. It disturbed me as well!

I was in third grade when I started to dream about making it to State tournament, this was in the 1969–70 basketball season. In the meantime, Dad would take us to all the Peerless games and the tournaments. I have a very clear memory of watching Robin Selvig lead the Outlook Blue Jays to win the District 1-C championship game that year against Antelope at the Plentywood High School Fieldhouse, where the District 1-C tournament was always held. Robin Selvig was a senior at Outlook that year. He went on to play for the Grizzlies of the University of Montana from 1970–1974 and has been head coach for the Lady Griz for the past 32 years. After District, Dad took Jon and me to watch the Divisional tournament. There I remember watching Outlook beat an excellent Saco team, led by Rocky Tollefson, 74–70 in a very close and exciting Divisional semi-final game. Robin's younger brother Randy, only a freshman then, came in and sparked Outlook to the victory with some key shots in the fourth quarter, on some fine assists from older brother Robin.

When Outlook went on to win Divisional the next night and make it to State, I remember listening to their games on the radio. At times the reception would vary from good to bad, but I could just feel the excitement of the crowd coming through the radio. Dad and Jon would be very excited as well. Outlook lost a very close game 67–64 to Hingham in the semi-finals (Robin Selvig scored 48 points that game) and was eliminated from the tournament in the Saturday morning game. As I was listening to the games on the radio, I believed our team could play at the State Class C tournament in Helena someday. I could only imagine how exciting it must be to play at State, since the games I had already seen at District and Divisional were so exciting. I began to form the fascinating image in my mind of how absolutely incredible it must be to play at State.

My third grade team, the Peerless Cougars of 1969–70, went 2–3, so Tiny Puckett's Cougars lost the first three games of their basketball careers, but finished the season strong with two wins. After we won our last game of the season against Opheim, Dad paraded up and down main street Opheim in our van with the Cougars banner draped across it, honking the horn in victory, much to the delight of all the Cougar boys in the van! The banner, made by Jon and me, showed a Cougar stomping all over a Viking.

Tiny Puckett and the 1970 Peerless Cougars, third grade.

Here are the results of the first season for Tiny Puckett and the Peerless Cougars:

> Opheim 13 Peerless 10
> Opheim 11 Peerless 9
> Scobey 37 Peerless 14
> Peerless 17 Opheim 7
> Peerless 19 Opheim 12

The 37–14 drubbing we took from Scobey was the worst loss I had in my ten year Cougar-Bobcat-Panther career, and it stuck with me for many years. I didn't like the feeling I had at the end of that game. After that, we finished the season strong, beating Opheim twice, the same team that had beaten us twice earlier in the season, learning from our previous losses and steadily improving as the season progressed, in typical Tiny Puckett fashion.

Tiny Puckett and the 1971 Peerless Cougars, fourth grade champs, 9-0.

Fourth Grade Champs

In fourth grade, our team, the Peerless Cougars, completed a perfect 9–0 record and won the season-ending tournament in Peerless against Whitetail. This was the first year when I really began to believe that our team could make it to State tournament. This was also the last year that we played in the old gym at Peerless, as we moved into our new gym the following year. It was exciting to know that we would be playing in a brand new gym the following year, but sad at the same time, because the old gym was where I'd had my first experiences with basketball, and I felt very comfortable playing

Jon Puckett with fourth grade championship trophy following championship game against Whitetail. Uncle Ed Puckett is seated to the left.

there. Here are the results of our games. Notice that Tiny Puckett
didn't take any prisoners.

> Peerless 35 Outlook 30
> Peerless 40 Outlook 22
> Peerless 45 Opheim 17
> Peerless 50 Flaxville 15
> Peerless 28 Flaxville (5th and 6th grade team) 25
> Peerless 44 Opheim 3
> Peerless 50 Saco 18
> Tournament at Peerless
> Whitetail 38 Opheim 27
> Peerless 41 Opheim 20
> Peerless 39 Whitetail 25 (championship)

When we went back to play at Flaxville after we beat their
fourth graders 50–15, the Flaxville principal would not allow another
drubbing, so he put us against their 5th and 6th grade team, and we

beat them! Ironically, the 50 points we scored against Flaxville in fourth grade would be the same amount of points we would score against them at State championship in 1979. Were we reaping some bad karma?

A Key Acquisition

The new gym and school that was built the year following my fourth grade season attracted a great family, with some great basketball players, to move to Peerless. I remember sitting at the kitchen table one day and Dad was so excited to tell me that Alfie Dighans and his family were moving to Peerless. Dad had played basketball with Alfie for many years on the Peerless Pirates, and he had four boys that could all play basketball: Mark, Scott, Bruce and Joel. So this was huge! I played high school basketball with Scott, Bruce and Joel, and Joel was our center on the 1978–79 teams that played at State. Scott was probably the best center to ever play at Peerless, and Bruce was a great forward on the 1975–1977 teams.

Fifth Grade Champs

In fifth grade, the 1971–72 season, our team also had a great season, winning the fifth grade championship, again against Whitetail. This was the last year my dad could coach us in basketball. Following the championship game, all of the players presented Tiny with a plaque that read: "He who seizes the right moment, is the right man", a quote by the German Johann Wolfgang von Goethe. Superintendent Marvin Hash was the man who had the idea for the language on the plaque, as none of us fifth graders were reading too much Goethe at the time! So Tiny Puckett went out a winner as a coach, but it was sad to think I wouldn't play for him again as my coach in basketball.

Later in that winter of 1972, I remember listening to the radio as Westby, led by center Neil Peterson, along with his brother Jim, and forward Les Leininger, won the State C tournament, the first year that a team from District 1-C had ever won the tournament. What was so fascinating about listening to those games on the radio was

Tiny Puckett and the 1972 Peerless Cougars, fifth grade champs.

that I had watched Westby play Peerless twice that year, and now here they were 450 miles away playing on the grandest stage of all, the Carroll College Physical Education Center in Helena, winning it all! Maybe someday that could be us?

A Giant Leap

In my seventh grade year, 1973–74, Peerless basketball took a giant leap forward. This was the first season since the high school was established in 1932 (41 years) that Peerless made it to the Divisional tournament, and we had to beat two good teams to do it. It wasn't something going into the tournament that I even thought was possible. Our high school team was playing the Lustre Lions in the first game, and trailed by one point with only seconds left to play when my older cousin Don Puckett stole the ball from Lustre's star player, Ron Reddig, and dribbled in for a layup to put us up by one point. We ended up winning that game after Lustre missed a last second shot.

The next night Peerless played a very good Antelope team, who the following year would take second at State, losing only to eventual State champion Westby. We were leading by 15–20 points very late in the game and our Coach, Marvin Hash, took the starters out of the game. I remember thinking, "It's too early! Something could still go wrong!" It was so incredulous that Peerless was finally going to advance to the championship game at District. We lost the championship game the following night to Westby, but we were heading onto Divisional, and that was something I will never forget, watching the Peerless Panthers play in their first ever District championship game.

At Divisionals I saw the "Greatest Shot in Peerless Basketball History," so coined by Kathleen Fladager. We were playing in the morning game against Nashua and were trailing by a single point with only seconds remaining. Nashua's best free throw shooter Mike Heikens was shooting a one and one but he missed the first one. Steve Miner then got the ball and shot it from just beyond half court on the right side. The ball banked in at the buzzer! That win put us in the consolation game at Divisionals, which we lost (again to Westby) but that placed Peerless fourth at Divisionals, the highest ever finish for a Peerless basketball team.

Eighth Grade Champs

The following season, 1974–75, I was an eighth grader, and our junior high team, the Bobcats, went 17–3 winning the end of season tournament against Craig Guenther's Antelope team. We won the game 59–29, playing incredible basketball. And that same year, the Peerless Panthers, after a drought of 41 years, advanced to Divisionals for the second year in a row, this time by upsetting the number one ranked team in the state, previously undefeated Westby, in the semi-final game at District. It was an incredible game for Peerless,

Coach Ron Scott and the 1975 Peerless Bobcats, eighth grade champs.

and I will never forget watching the end of that game, as our star player, Duane "Duke" Trangsrud held the ball out of bounds with three seconds left and Westby was forced to watch helplessly as the clock wound down, as they were out of timeouts. Westby would go on to win the State tournament that year, with Antelope taking second, a 1–2 finish for District 1-C at State in 1975. Westby was led by Alan Nielsen and David Shields and a great supporting cast of role players. Antelope had an amazing starting five of Keith Ueland and Harvey Lee at forwards, Les Hovet at center, and Vic Johansen and Dennis Guenther at guards. Harold Ming was a great sixth man. If it weren't for Westby that year, Antelope would have won the State championship. It was also in 1975 that Medicine Lake, led by center Rod Smith and Brent Leibach (only a sophomore at the time), won the State Class B tournament. They would come down to rejoin District 1-C in 1976–77, in Brent Leibach's senior year.

Peerless Panthers the morning after their upset of #1 Westby, 1975.

Disappointment and Frustration

My high school basketball career began the following year in the 1975–76 season. We had a very good team that year, led by our star center, 6'4" Scott Dighans. In 1976, we lost to a fine Outlook team on Friday night at District, then lost out to Antelope the next morning. We had taken third in the conference that year and were expected to make it to Divisional again, but did not play well at District. Flaxville won the District, Divisional and State championship that year, all for the first time in the school's history. They had an incredibly tall and talented team, with good guard play. They started Keith Hatfield 6'3" and brother Kevin Hatfield 6'7", at forwards. Blaine Kurtz was 6'5" at center, and Craig Miller 5'10" and Tully Tryan 5'10" at guards. This team, coached by Rod Wiemeri, had more height, depth and balance than any Class C team I ever saw, with David Safty 6'6" and Thor Gunderson 6'3" coming off the bench. The Superintendent of Flaxville for this year of firsts for the

Cardinals was Rip Holo.

The following year, my sophomore year, Bruce Dighans' and Ross Chapman's senior year, we took second in conference but lost a tough double-overtime game to Westby 72–70 at District semi-finals. Then we were knocked out of the tournament again by Antelope in the morning. This was a frustrating time for the Panthers: Having had a little taste of success in 1974 and 1975, it became a disappointing season when the Panthers didn't even make it to divisional, especially when we really expected to go. These were my first two years in high school! So, after all the success playing as a younger boy with the Cougars and Bobcats, I had completed my sophomore year in high school and had yet to even get out of District. After the 1977 losses at District, the dream of making it to State seemed very, very distant indeed.

The Perfect Storm

But then came my junior year, 1977–78 , when the Panthers became the first Peerless team to ever make it to the State tournament. At the time, I thought the experience was solely about the basketball players on the court winning game, but now that I look back on it over 30 years later, I realize the players were simply a part of something much bigger than themselves or even the game of basketball. It was about community, leadership, coaching, prior successful teams, hard work and discipline, and last, but certainly not least, a new gymnasium.

Without the community (and our cheerleaders and pep club) behind us, supporting us, cheering us on, believing in us, there would be nothing backing up all the effort, nothing to pick us up when we got down. The support of the community gave us players the feeling that we were just not playing for ourselves. People cared about how we did, and they won and lost with us on the court. Without this support, we would have been out there all alone. The 1977–78 Panthers, as did all the Peerless teams before them and since, had the unwavering *support* of the Peerless Community.

Leadership is paramount: Marvin Hash, the coach of the 1974

team that made it to Divisional for the first time in school history, as well as the Superintendent of Peerless Schools, was a great leader. There were times I didn't like him, but I always respected him. I got in trouble a few times while I was in high school and was disciplined for it. Probably one of the greatest things Marvin Hash's leadership taught us was that nothing could really be accomplished without discipline. He was old school and he ran a tight ship. Many people disagreed with him and his methods, but in the end, the Peerless School was disciplined, and the basketball teams under his tenure (whether Superintendent or coach or both) reflected this discipline on the court.

Excellent coaching is crucial: Marvin Hash (1971–74), Ron Scott (1974–1976) and Clark Shaffer (1976–1978) were all great coaches. Something amazing was their vastly different styles. Marvin Hash was a great disciplinarian. I remember watching his first practice in the new gym with the high school team and my jaw dropped. Players had to say "Yes Sir!" "No Sir!" to him when they talked to him— stuff like that, which I hadn't seen before with the previous coaches. It was quite a change. He had control of the practices. He wasn't an exceptional player himself, nor was he a mastermind with strategy, but man could he motivate players and get them to play together as a team.

Ron Scott was an amazing coach (and player!) He was very stern, as he emphasized and taught the fundamentals of defense like no other coach I had ever seen. Several of us players that played on that 1977–1978 State team had him as our coach in junior high, where he taught us how to play team defense and execute a good offensive set as a team. We had a level of coaching in junior high school that many players never got in high school, and (I would venture to say) even in college if they went that far.

Then came Clark Shaffer—a sharp contrast to his predecessor Ron Scott, to say the least. Clark was young, just out of Carroll College. Although he didn't have much experience coaching, he was a great coach just the same. The one obvious gift that Clark Shaffer had was that he knew how to relate to his players. Actually, I think it just came naturally to him. It wasn't something he tried to do, it was just his personality. He was easy going, funny and would tell jokes that always kept us loose. He used to say things like, "It doesn't matter if you win or lose, as long as you look good." Then he'd explain to us how we really needed to wear our socks lower, not pull them up so high because it didn't look cool! We worked hard in practice, but he made practices fun; rarely, if ever, did he yell at a player. But he didn't need to. We all wanted to play for him because we really liked him, and we were just having fun playing basketball. One of the drills we did at the end of the last practice before a game was called "Shooting out of your ass" Each player would dribble up the court and then make up a funny, wild shot, maybe imitating another player on another team or just make a shot up. The assistant coach, Brian Bechtold, (also young and funny) would crack up when he'd see a funny shot. Shaffer coached a motion passing game offense that was perfect for our guard-oriented team. It was just a perfect match. We had already learned all the fundamentals and discipline we needed from Marvin Hash and Ron Scott (not that Shaffer didn't teach these things too, he did) but now it was time to apply all of that in our passing game offense, and (quite simply) just have fun playing basketball.

Prior successful teams: The 1974 team that made it to Divisional for the first time, and then did well when they got there, and the 1975 team that upset Westby at District and made it to Divisional again, caused the younger Peerless kids to believe that success was possible. Watching these teams play and make it to Divisional made us believe that we could do it too, and they paved the way for the successful teams that followed them.

Hard work and discipline: I'm not sure Jon and I had a strong work-ethic; we definitely had a strong play-ethic. We just loved to play the game of basketball, and we were both very competitive, something our dad had instilled in us growing up. Whenever we would go together to the gym to play basketball, we would start out by each shooting on one side of the court opposite the other. This started in the old gym when we were six or seven years old when we would go up there at night with Dad in the winter, and carried on when we moved into the new gym when we had our own key and could go up there ourselves. I remember watching Jon shoot on the other side of the court. He would usually shoot from the baseline, which I always wondered about because he was a guard; it was forwards who usually shot from the baseline. Most of the shots I practiced were from the top of the key or to the left or right of it. If you were to chart shots from our games, you'd probably see a lot of Jon's shots coming from the baseline, whereas, most of mine would have been from around the top of the key.

After shooting around for a half hour or so, we would play one on one. I don't know why or how it came to be, but all of our one on one games were up to 60 points, by ones. One point for each basket made, make it take it after the third basket was made. This meant that the player who made their third basket kept the ball on offense until the defender made a stop. Some days we would play a single game up to 60, but we would usually end up playing a best of three game series and span the series across a couple days. This would happen because the loser of the first game would ask the other twin, "Want to play the best two out of three?" Sometimes we would extend a series to the best of five games, or even the best of seven games, and span it across several days, just as if it were the NBA playoffs. These one on one games were very competitive and each series usually went to the final game, while most of the games ended up like 60–56, 60–58. Which meant, if one were to keep track, that in a seven game series spanning several days, each of us would have made around 350–400 shots, most of them under pressure. Oh, and you had to win by two, so some of our games would go over 60 points! These "practice" sessions we did would sometimes last three or four hours. And we loved every minute of it. It was a play-ethic.

I've been writing about all the things that had to be in place for Peerless to make it to State that year. The "Perfect Storm" that had to come together. So far, it's been community, leadership, coaching, prior successful teams and hard work and discipline. But last, and certainly not least, was the new gymnasium. Dad always talked about how difficult it was for Peerless teams to do well at District because the old gym was so small. It was hard for the players to adjust to the bigger court when they had practiced on the smaller court all year long. It was a severe disadvantage. We all loved the old gym but it wasn't the best court to prepare for the winning of tournaments. So, when the new gym opened in the fall of 1971, a new era in Peerless basketball had begun. It was only three years later that Peerless made it to Divisional for the first time, never having been there previously.

So, these were all of the things that had to be in place for the dream to come true. It was about so much more than just our team, than about basketball. It was about the entire Peerless community, and all of us were a part of it, and always will be.

The Ride to State in '78

Bloody Noses

So in the previous two seasons of 1976 and 1977, my freshman and sophomore years, we had suffered two bitterly disappointing losses at District tournament and had not advanced to Divisionals, which brings us to the 1978 Panthers, my junior year. We were not a dominant team in 1978. Going into the District tourney, our record was 13–7, and we had taken a dismal fourth place in the conference with a 6–4 record. We were playing in another ridiculously tough 1-C conference, and had lost twice to Flaxville, once to Outlook and once to Westby. In non-conference games, we had lost three times to a very good Scobey team, a team that should have made it to State that year in class B, but did win it the following year, losing only one game the entire year. So, having placed fourth place in the conference, it seemed like we were faced yet again with the prospect of not advancing out of our District tournament, let alone achieving the goal of making it to State. This was a very frustrating situation for us to be in, as our team of destiny was not realizing its goal. Then, what followed next was an absolutely unbelievable, unforgettable tournament run, culminated by a spectacular finish at the State tournament in Helena, complete with a fairy tale ending.

The one silver lining in our 13–7 record was that we had lost only to good teams, and we had become a better team as a result. One of the things Dad always said was, "you always play to the level of your competition." When we were at a very young age, like eight

1978 Peerless Panthers.

1978 Panther Cheerleaders. Daniels County Leader photo.

and nine years old, he would schedule games against Little League teams in baseball where the kids were eleven and twelve years old. I mean, good teams too. He did the same thing in basketball. In many cases we were playing against kids that were three to four years older than us. He'd always say before the game, "Well boys, we're going to get our noses a little bloody against these guys," or "We're going to get our feet wet", and in some cases, literally, we got our noses bloody! Normally we would get pounded. I remember walking out onto the field when we were nine years old against a Frazer little league team that consisted only of 12-year-olds. I recall the Frazer players (and fans) looking at us and saying as we walked onto the field, "They're all so *little!*" Jon and I struggled to get the ball over the plate the required 45 feet, and whenever we did, the ball usually came smack back at us. I felt like Charlie Brown on the mound sometimes. But you know what? Later in the year we would circle back and play that same team, and we would do a little better, and a little better still if we played them again. In some few cases, at the end of the season, we would beat the same team that pounded us earlier in the year. The reason I relate this is because the 1977–78 Peerless Panthers had gotten their noses bloodied a lot that year (seven times to be exact) and we were a lot better team—a lot tougher team—going into District tourney because of it. We were not afraid to take the court against anyone. Who says there is nothing to be learned from a loss?

The Tension Mounts

The path to Divisional for Peerless that year had to go through Outlook, the eventual State champion, and ranked in the top ten teams in state for much of the year. They were the conference champion and we were headed for a showdown with them on semi-final night at District. They had a great team with Dave and Doug Selvig, Randy Wangerin, Jerry West (no relation to the Laker, but you might have thought he was!) and their young center, Les Sebastian. You knew if you had to play a team with *two* Selvigs on it you were in trouble! Are you kidding me?

Do you remember the movie, "Three Men and a Baby?" Outlook was sort of like "Four Guards and a Center". They gave us fits because they continuously countered our guard play—they had an answer for it. But we gave them fits too, because, well, we were basically "Five Guards and No Center"! Joel Dighans, a sophomore who played center for us was maybe 5'11" at the time, but he played like he was about 6'4". We had beaten Outlook once at home earlier that year 56–54, then had lost to them embarrassingly at Outlook only three weeks before the District tourney by 16 points, but we were never really in the game. They had blown us out, as Outlook

Joe Puckett shoots as Doug Selvig and Les Sebastian defend.
Peerless at Outlook, three weeks before District tournament, 1978.

often did to opponents on their home court. We were headed for a third showdown with them on semi-final night at District. It would be a shootout.

We were anxious for the tourney to begin, but bad weather (that would be snow) set in and the tournament was delayed until the following week, on Monday. This gave us more time to think about it. The pressure was building. I remember looking at Jon and thinking, "This is our junior year in high school and we have yet to even get out of our own District. All of those hours in the gym, all of the practices, all of the one-on-ones we've played, all of the hard work . . ." We had doubts. Then, after we thought about it, we realized it was very simple: If we were going to get out of our District for the first time in our high school career, we were just going to have to beat the best team in the state to do it! (Hmmm, I seem to recall a Peerless team that had done that before?) Once we accepted what we had to do, it seemed to become easier. At home one night a few days before the tourney, Jon took out a piece of school paper, and with a pen he outlined one word, one very large word, colored it in darkly, and taped it to the wall in our bedroom. The one word written on the page was: WIN. Seems the Panthers were a little hungry . . .

Pronghorn Revenge

There is an advantage, a very solid advantage, I think, for *not* having a bye in a tournament. You get to work the kinks out, get loose, get a feel for the court and get the butterflies out the first night, rather than running onto the court the second night for the first time and playing a team who has already done what you now need to do. The first night at District that year we played fifth place Antelope. We had a little revenge factor, as Antelope had knocked us out of District in both 1976 and 1977. We had handled them easily during the season, and had our way with them in the tournament too. It was great to get a big lead early. We relaxed and just played Peerless basketball, running up and down the court, fast breaking, working our passing game offense to perfection and pressuring the ball on defense. The thing about Antelope that year was, their best player, Craig Guenther, a junior, had transferred to Plentywood following his sophomore season at Antelope. The year before, in 1977, he led Antelope to the Divisional championship and a State tourney berth, after their team took last in the conference. Antelope didn't do well at State in 1977 because Craig Guenther was sick and couldn't play at State. The following year, 1978, the year we made it to State, Guenther led Plentywood to the State Class B championship and was named the MVP of the tourney. His Plentywood team had beaten Scobey three times that year; Scobey was a team that had beaten us three times! This is how tough 1-C was back then. I don't even want to think about what our conference would have been like in 1978 with Guenther in it!

The win against Antelope brought on the confrontation with Outlook, on a weird Tuesday night at Plentywood. Plentywood's gym was usually packed for a semi-final at District, especially if a Sheridan County team was playing, which Outlook was. But this night it was unusually packed because fans from District 2-C were there as well, people from places like Culbertson and Froid, because they weren't playing their District tournament during the week. There were a lot of letterman jackets with colors you normally didn't see at Plentywood at a 1-C game. The fieldhouse was buzzing with expectation because Peerless and Outlook played a style of basket-ball that was so much fun to watch: Short, quick players with great ball handling skills, sharp outside shooters that played fast break basketball, and pressure man-to-man defense. With the exception of Les Sebastian, Outlook's 6'3" center, a Peerless-Outlook matchup was like watching a six-foot-and-under tournament. Actually, it was like watching an under-six-foot tournament! We didn't have a single six-foot player on our team! Each team was fun to watch by themselves, but I think it was an extra treat for the fans to watch the teams play each other.

And the teams didn't disappoint. As expected, both teams came out firing and the shootout was on . . .

A Fine Tradition

Before we get into the shootout, however, I need to mention a couple things about Outlook basketball. Of all the teams in 1-C, a District with a fine basketball tradition, Outlook was the finest. They had a tradition of winning, of marvelous athletes, great coaches, and a fan-base that had an absolute passion for and knowledge of the game of basketball. I remember playing them at the new Peerless gym when I was a fifth-grader, one of the first games I remember playing there. Randy Wangerin, Jerry West and Dave Selvig were sixth-graders; they were seniors in 1978. I had never before seen basketball played the way they played it. It was brilliant. They beat the crap out of us. Towards the end of the game I was tired and frustrated; I got bumped to the floor by someone and started crying. As I mentioned before, Dad had always scheduled games against tougher opponents; we were used to getting pounded, but not like this. But apparently, as badly as they beat us, our style of ball had made an impression on them as well. After the game, I remember Jerry West and Randy Wangerin came into our locker room; they told me I had played a great game and asked if I was ok. I was surprised to see them. I told them I was fine, but that I just didn't like to lose. And, almost in unison, they replied, "That's ok, we don't like to lose either." I remember thinking as I watched them walk out of the locker room door, "I want to play on a team as good as that someday." And someday I would.

I don't remember too many games where I got frustrated like that, but the ones I do remember were all against Outlook. On their home court, they could blow you out of a game in the first quarter. I mean, the game would be over *before* the end of the first quarter. You didn't even want to come back out onto the court and play anymore. They could break your spirit. On the far end of their court, they put chairs up on the stage behind the basket where their pep club sat (stood, jumped). The cheerleaders were on the court in front of them, just to the side of the basket, and they were absolutely raucous. For some reason, it seemed like we would always be defending this basket in the first half, and it felt like the cheerleaders and pep club were on the court with the team, and like there were about eight or nine Blue Jays in uniform on the court, running circles around us. If you turned your head on defense for a split-second, they were behind you shooting a layup with a sharp pass or pulling up for a wide-open jump shot. They would start with a full court press and swarm the ball, get steals and then attack the basket before you could recover. If you did manage to break the press and get the ball to the other side of the court, they would fast break you to death coming the other way, with three-on-ones and two-on-ones. It was like blitzkrieg on the court, with the pep club and cheerleaders in your face as shots rained down all around you. The Outlook team that we were playing at District that night was that explosive. You had to be very careful against this team; make sure you marked your man, kept them in front of you, saw both the ball and your man, took care of the ball, and didn't let them come out and take the game away from you in the first quarter. In the game that we had played at Outlook only three weeks prior to District, they led us 41–15 late in the first half. At halftime, we managed to get the score to a respectable 41–19. Yeah.

Another thing about Outlook basketball was its tradition of having fine coaches. In 1978, Rollie Sullivan was their head coach, and he was a very good coach. Tough, old school, get-in-your-grill kind of a coach. Actually, I can't remember an Outlook coach that didn't have this style! He was also a great strategist. But you don't have to take my word for it that he was a good coach; I have evidence that can't be disputed: He was dating Sandy Selvig at the time, and there is no way any Selvig would be seen with someone who didn't absolutely know basketball. It just wouldn't work. So there you have it: Rollie Sullivan was a good coach.

But on this particular night, Rollie Sullivan, a great coach representing a long line of great coaches from Outlook, would get out-coached by young Clark Shaffer. Shaffer, who had recently graduated from Carroll College two years prior, was only in his second year as head coach at Peerless.

The Achilles Heel

Every team has an Achilles Heel. No matter how good or seemingly invincible they might be, they have a weakness. For Peerless that year, it was no secret what our Achilles Heel was: defending inside and rebounding against taller teams. You could just say defending inside and rebounding against *every* team we played, because *every* team we played was taller than us. You could look at Peerless, not even actually see the team, but just look at their lineup in the tournament program, and see 5'9", 5'8", 5'10", 5'9", 5'11" (oh, that must be their center!), 5'7" and so on. You could keep going down the list of players and never see a height that began with a six! Peerless wore its weakness on its sleeve; we were transparent, and other teams knew exactly what they had to do to beat us: Get us in a slow, half court, methodical inside game, as opposed to a fast, open-court, improvisational perimeter game, the game we loved to play. Actually this is the game Outlook loved to play too, with one exception: They had an inside game. They had a center, and Jerry West and Doug Selvig were both great rebounders, so their inside game, while not exceptional, was not weak.

So did Outlook have an Achilles Heel? We looked at the team and we couldn't see one. Certainly it wasn't their guard play, got that covered. Not their inside game, as already mentioned. They could play inside, outside, pass, shoot, defend, rebound. They were well coached. They all played smart. Did they have a weakness? I'm not sure anyone watching them play that night could see they had a weakness, but I think one man knew what it was: Clark Shaffer.

The Shootout Begins

The game started out fast and furious, as expected. Outlook came out, as they always did, very aggressive and pushing the game to us. I remember thinking, "Just don't let the first few minutes of this game get out of hand, keep an eye on your man, get back on defense, and help out your teammates." The 41–15 score at Outlook three weeks earlier was still fresh in our minds. So in the beginning of the game, our team was more focused on defense, controlling their attack. Later on, in the second quarter, our focus would switch more to offense, after we had controlled their initial push, survived the initial salvos. After an up-and-down first quarter, the Blue Jays led 16–11. This was a low point total for Peerless that year for any quarter, but we weren't shooting that bad, we were just focused on the defensive side of the court. Interestingly, there was one little statistic at the end of the first quarter that I don't think anyone gave much attention to: Dave Selvig, Outlook's leader, playmaker, best defender and sharpshooter, had two fouls. I think Clark Shaffer was paying attention.

Outlook came out strong to start the second quarter, scoring on a fast break and then pushing the lead to 19–11. I remember thinking, "This is dangerous, don't want to let this go any further, better pick it up on offense." It was time to attack. We were slipping behind, but Outlook was not playing on their home court this time. It was different. Now, it was our turn.

Recalling the brilliant second quarter Peerless had unleashed just three years earlier against number one Westby on the same court, the Panthers broke out. We started raining jump shots from all over the court. Roger Trang, Bernie Wasser, Joel Dighans, Bill Fladager, Jon and I, we all started to light it up. Outlook was matching it with their sharp shooting too, and then the crowd that had been waiting for the shootout to begin in earnest, really started to come alive. The Peerless crowd, who had been relatively calm in the first quarter, suddenly became electric. With each successive jump shot, they got louder and louder. Outlook's crowd was wild too, and pretty soon the entire gym was rocking. I remember we were shooting at the basket on the left side of the gym. The Peerless crowd, at least when we played at District, always sat on the bottom part of the bleachers on this left side, so our crowd was on the same side of the court we where were shooting, very close to us. Now, unlike three weeks earlier at Outlook, it felt like *they* were on the court with us. I usually never looked at the crowd when I played because it was a distraction, but I remember this time I actually had to look over at our crowd to check it out because they were so crazy. We started to really feed off of them. This was the true beginning of the wild ride to State in 1978. When we started to play like that in the second quarter, it was like the Peerless fans stood up and never sat down again until we got back from Helena after it was all over. This Peerless crowd, which later on would pick up a lot more Peerless fans on the tournament trail to Helena, was a *huge* reason for our success. This was the community support I mentioned earlier. Everyone in Peerless was a part of the experience, and a part of the reason our team was able to do what it did.

A Big Mistake

Meanwhile, in the middle of all this excitement, Dave Selvig, Outlook's leader and playmaker, picked up his third foul. In the games we had played against Outlook previously that year they had never gotten in foul trouble, so this was something new. They played smartly on defense and didn't get stupid fouls. I remember I was excited because this meant he would be coming out of the game for the last part of the second quarter. But he didn't come out! Rollie Sullivan left him in the game! What? The decision Rollie apparently made was that with the momentum Peerless had at that point he couldn't afford to take Dave out. But this was a huge, huge risk. If Dave picked up his fourth foul in the first half, he could be ineffective the rest of the game, on the edge of fouling out on every play, and this would be devastating for Outlook. Coach Shaffer recognized this and started to call specific plays on offense attacking Dave. Dave had switched from defending me, which he usually did, to defending Jon, and Coach Shaffer started to target Jon for isolation on Dave. And sure enough, late in the second quarter, with only a few seconds left in the half, Dave Selvig picked up his fourth foul guarding Jon. Jon made both free throws and we led 36–33 at halftime. The chink in Outlook's armor had been exposed: They had no depth. Five good players, but not six. Coach Shaffer knew this and had exploited the big mistake Rollie Sullivan made, and there is no doubt but that Coach Sullivan's mistake—and Coach Shaffer's capitalization of it—would ultimately cost Outlook the game. Coach Shaffer had out-coached Rollie Sullivan. There were only a few seconds left in the first half when Dave got his fourth foul, but it would be in the next 16 minutes where the devastating effects of this would be realized for Outlook . . .

The Shootout, Part Two

When ten players—five Blue Jays and five Panthers— ran out onto the court to start the second half, Dave Selvig was not among them. Coach Sullivan had decided to sit him out for the entire third quarter. Of course, Coach Shaffer didn't know at halftime that Rollie was going to do this, so our strategy was basically if Dave was back in the game to attack him on offense; if he was out of the game, the strategy was to attack whomever it was that replaced him. But we also made some adjustments on defense. Dave was an incredible ball handler. Randy Wangerin, Outlook's other guard, could also handle the ball very well, but nothing like Dave. He was a tremendous shooter, could light it up, but Dave managed the court. So we started to put a little pressure on their guards upfront, which we usually didn't do against them, and it bothered them. But the biggest factor about Dave not being in the game was emotional, psychological. For Outlook, they were playing without their leader, and they were behind, a situation they weren't accustomed to for much of that season. For us, we were very confident that without him on the court we could do some things we couldn't normally do, and could control the game. And we did.

And then there was the crowd.

As if the gym wasn't packed enough when the game started, more people had come in at halftime because we were playing the first semi-final game. A lot of the Flaxville and Westby people were just then arriving for the second game. I'm not sure the Peerless crowd sat down at halftime; they just kept standing. It is hard to describe the atmosphere in the gym other than to say it was purely electric. We had lit it up for 25 points in the span of about seven minutes in the second quarter—over a 100-point game clip—and Outlook was playing well, too. Both teams had to be shooting well over 50%. Every fan in the gym was anticipating a second half like the first. This was Class C basketball at its best on a Tuesday night in Plentywood.

In the third quarter, the two teams kept running up and down the court, trading baskets as the shootout continued. We shot an incredible percentage from the field; all of us continued to shoot well, and, just like in the first half, the crowd kept getting louder and louder. I keep saying that, but I had never before played in a gym where it was even close to being that loud. This time, the Peerless crowd was behind us, to the right as we attacked up the court. Our pep club and cheerleaders were behind us on the far end of the court to the left when were on offense. Every time we made a basket, I could feel a roar behind me that would almost blow me off my feet. Our team was playing at a level far above that which we had played at all year, and it was fantastic. And, again, it was the crowd that was lifting us up. And it wasn't just the Peerless and Outlook fans that were rowdy. You know the old Irish saying, "Is this is a private fight or can anyone join?" No one could sit there and simply observe this game.

At the end of every quarter, if we had possession of the ball and the lead, we would go for the last shot. Jon and I would watch the clock, and if we had the lead and the clock was under a minute, Coach Shaffer would usually have us go for the last shot. In this case, we were ahead by three points, and the clock got under a minute. We were going for the last shot. We would either go into the fourth quarter ahead by three points or ahead by five points. Going for the last shot, Jon or I would dribble to one side of the court and pass to a forward, usually either Bill or Roger; they'd pass it back out, and we'd switch the ball to the other side of the court and do the same thing. Sometimes Jon and I just dribbled back and forth up top and passed it back and forth to each other. No one came out to bother us as we did this because all of us, all five Panthers, could handle the ball. Then, with about ten to twelve seconds left, we would start our offense. In this game, Jon dribble penetrated and passed off to Joel Dighans for the last shot of the quarter. It went in with just a couple seconds left. The roar was *deafening*. The Panthers were going into the fourth quarter with a five-point lead, the

Joel Dighans shoots a free throw late in the third quarter
of District semi-final against Outlook, 1978.

momentum, and a Peerless crowd that had now just taken it through
the roof. And, as was the case three years earlier against Westby,
another upset was brewing semi-final night in Plentywood . . .

The Great Escape

When the fourth quarter began, Outlook, on paper at least, had to
be feeling pretty good about the situation, considering they had
played the entire third quarter without Dave Selvig, and had only
fallen behind by two more points than at halftime. He had scored 12
points in the first half, and now they had him back in the game. But
statistics can lie. After the shot went in at the end of the third
quarter, we had the crowd and the momentum. Dave had been
sitting on the bench the entire third quarter and had gotten out of
the flow of the game. And the flow of this game was like a locomo-
tive at full steam. When he came back in he wasn't the same player.
He also played a little tentatively because he didn't want to pick up
his fifth foul. He would only score one point in the fourth quarter,
and he quietly fouled out with about a minute and a half left.

The fourth quarter brought on more up-and-down play, the two teams trading baskets, shooting a torrid percentage. The gym was swelling with more noise as each shot went in. We were content to trade blows with Outlook because we had the lead, and slowly, gradually, we began to pull away. In every upset I can remember playing in, there comes a tipping point in the game where you start to believe, *really* believe, that you're going to win, and then a shot of adrenaline just launches you into the next level. This was the biggest ever upset for me (so far!) We had Outlook on the ropes and had expanded our lead to up to eight points. The time was running down in the game, and then Jon hit a long jump shot from the right side of the court, from the baseline, pushing our lead higher and the crowd into a frenzy. He ran down the court with his right index finger raised high in the air, signaling that the upset was real, that it was over, that the Panthers had done it again! The Peerless Panthers had upset the eventual State champion semi-final night at District again! Oh my! And more importantly, the Peerless Panthers of 1978, after two previous heart-breaking, frustrating years, had escaped from District 1-C and were moving on to Divisional . . .

Sky High

The greatest part about a big upset like that is the locker room afterwards. Tears were streaming down both Jon's face and mine. After two frustrating years of losing out at District we had finally cleared the hurdle and "escaped" from 1-C. The locker room was crazy, and I remember a lot of the Peerless fans, Dad being one of them, of course, came into share in the jubilation. I think Marvin Hash might have given us a rousing congratulatory speech. I can't describe how it felt. The closest word that I can come up with would be euphoria. Sky High.

   After we showered and dressed and got ready to leave the gym, I realized, "Hey, wait a minute, there's another game left to play here." We were in the championship game. And I also thought, seriously, "What's the point? We're going to Divisional, let's just pack up now and go to Wolf Point. Let the other teams play for third place to see who that is and that will be that." Third place would end up being Outlook. Later that night, Flaxville beat Westby in the other semi-final game and that meant the championship game would be an all Daniels County affair, the first time in the history of District 1-C that this had occurred. This was Flaxville's third consecutive appearance in the championship game; they had won the previous two in 1976 and 1977, going onto win State in 1976. The previous year, 1977, they had only lost one game the entire year, then lost to Antelope (who had taken last place in 1-C conference that year) in the Divisional final, and then to Richey in the challenge game Monday night. They had an exceptionally good team. We had lost to them twice during the season, including our homecoming game at Peerless. They were tall and had good guards, and played really good defense. Not really a lot of weaknesses there either.

The Evening After

Well, Flaxville was not the team to play with a "just happy to be here" mindset. A year later, in 1979, playing against Flaxville again for the District championship, our mindset would be completely different. We were shooting for our school's first ever District championship, but this year we were glad—elated—just to get out of District 1-C.

So, in the District championship game, Flaxville continued their mastery of us. In my three-year high school career, we had never beaten them; the loss to them in the championship game on this night would be our seventh straight loss to them. When I was a freshman in 1976, they won the State championship. In that year, they had an incredible front line of 6'7", 6'6" and 6'5". They had good guards, too. But what was amazing about their 1976 team was a freshman, 6'7" Kevin Hatfield—now a junior—was named the State C MVP at Helena. As a 14-year-old freshman! To my knowledge, that had never happened before and hasn't happened since. He was a tremendous player. They had good guards, too, in Wade and Cory Tryan. And, like every team in 1-C back then, they were extremely well coached. Terry Bakken was their coach, and he had

Joel Dighans and Kevin Hatfield tipoff,
District 1-C championship, Peerless vs. Flaxville, 1978.

previously coached at Antelope, leading them to a second place finish at State to Westby in 1975, and then back to State again in 1977. In 1975, the only team Antelope lost to the entire season was Westby.

In the championship game against Flaxville, we were so emotionally drained from the previous night's upset of Outlook that it took us awhile to adjust to the fact that we were even playing again. And we had to adjust to a completely different style of play as well. Flaxville had good guards, but they played ball control; they didn't run. They played a half court game and got it inside to their big guys underneath, exploiting their height advantage against us. Defensively, they never let us get into our open court game, because they would pound it inside and their guards would always be back on defense. Our pressure defense on the press normally didn't bother them, as their guards were able to handle our pressure. They led at every quarter break and won going away, 61–46, completely dominating us in the second half. It was by far the lowest point total ever for Peerless that season. In many cases, we would score 46 points in a single half. Kevin Hatfield led them with 18 points. It was tough to swallow; just 24 hours earlier we were sky high after the upset against Outlook. But now we were down, puzzled by the fact that this team had dominated us yet again, as they had done since I was a freshman, and we couldn't seem to find an answer for it.

But the pain wore off fairly quickly. We were headed to Divisional for the first time in my high school career, and we would see this team again. Oh yes, we would see this team again! And with much higher stakes on the line, and a much different outcome, as the incredible, unbelievable Ride to State in 1978 continued . . .

The Trifecta

Because of the blizzard, we had played our District tourney on Monday through Wednesday. So on that weekend, some of us went to watch District 3-C tourney in Glasgow. As I watched the teams play in that tourney, I knew our chances were good at Divisional; these teams were not nearly as strong as the 1-C teams that season.

At halftime of the District 3-C championship game at Glasgow, I was standing next to a referee who had refereed the game we had played at Hinsdale a week before our tournament. We had beaten them badly (our record outside of 1-C that year was 7–0), and I overheard the ref tell his buddy, "It doesn't matter who makes it out of this District, they're all just going to get the shit kicked out of them at Divisional anyway." The teams from 2-C that had watched Peerless-Outlook and Westby-Flaxville at our District semi-final night knew when they left the gym that night they weren't going to get out of Divisional either. So for the trifecta bet going into Divisional that year, it was not hard to pick who the top three teams would be, but in what order they would finish. It was going to be Outlook, Flaxville and Peerless in the top three, but who would Win, Place, and Show? The team that Showed was not going to State. Which team would it be?

We ploughed through our bracket at Divisional. One of the great things about losing to Flaxville in the championship at District (yes, I do mean "great") was that we were placed in the bracket opposite Outlook and Flaxville at Divisional. They "got" to play each other semi-final night. We beat Frazer 70–62 the first night and then beat a very good Richey team semi-final night in a blowout 72–51. It was just too easy. After having struggled simply to get out of 1-C for two years, we were expecting a little more of a challenge out of Divisional.

Well, we were going to get that challenge. Outlook had defeated Flaxville 61–58 in the semi-final game, and Flaxville had come back to win the consolation game against Richey, setting up the expected 1–2–3 finish for 1-C at Divisional. So, when we ran onto the court to play Outlook for the championship game at Divisional—the first time in history a Peerless team had played for the Divisional championship—we knew two things: If we beat Outlook, we were going to the State tournament for the first time in the school's history; if we lost, we were going to have to face Flaxville, our nemesis, a team that had beaten us seven straight times, had owned

Joel Dighans shoots over Rolly Starkey of Richey, Divisional semi-final, 1978.

and dominated us, in a challenge game on Monday night. We really didn't want to lose to Outlook.

The Rematch

Just like at District against Outlook, the Wolf Point gym was packed that night. As I mentioned previously, we picked up a lot more fans along the tourney ride to Helena that year. In this case, it was local fans from Wolf Point who really enjoyed our open-court, fast-break style of basketball. This was the and last time we would play Outlook that year, and (amazingly) we had beaten them twice. They only lost four games all year and two of them were to us.

It seemed like we had steamrolled into the championship game so fast that there wasn't much time to think about where we were. My lifelong dream of making it to State for the first time was now a looming possibility, but I don't remember thinking about it much before the game. Outlook, on the other hand, had been there before. Not this team, but previous teams, and that makes a difference. Robin Selvig and Randy Selvig's teams had both played in this game in 1970 and 1973 (and won it), and now it was Dave's (and Doug's, only a sophomore at this time) turn. It was going to be another tough game against Outlook.

Seems like no matter how much we prepared for Outlook's initial assault out of the gate that year, we couldn't stop it, and that was the case yet again in the championship game. They were playing brilliantly in the first quarter, and were lighting it up from all over the court on long-range jump shots and fast break lay-ups. We found ourselves behind by ten points and then ended the first quarter behind by eight.

But we kept our poise—probably because we had seen them three times before—and gradually began to chip away at their lead. Oddly, the game turned into more of a half court game after the first quarter. It was still fast, but both teams were so wary of each other's fast break that the defenses were not allowing the other team to get into the open court. Then, mid-way through the second quarter, it happened again, just like at District. Dave Selvig picked up his third

Joel Dighans and Les Sebastian tipoff,
Divisional championship, Peerless vs. Outlook, 1978

foul, again guarding Jon. And this time, before the ref had raised his hand to hold up Dave's number, signaling the foul, Rollie Sullivan already had a sub on the bench ready to come in for Dave. He wasn't going to make the same mistake he had made at District twice. I think Roald Selvig, father Selvig, was actually on his way down to the bench from his seat in the gym to ensure that didn't happen.

Executing our half court passing game offense and playing solid defense, we slowly began to chip away at the lead. We were down seven at halftime and by two points at the end of the third quarter. The crowd was going nuts! Eight minutes to go to State! Now I started to think about it.

The fourth quarter was back and forth, each team executing its half court offense. We had improved so much as a team in the tournament, playing far better than we had all year—on another level, really. We had never led the entire game, and then late in the fourth quarter, trailing by three points and in possession of the ball, I remember Bill Fladager (a great passer, a role player) gave me a perfect pass. It was a back door play called by Coach Shaffer and we used to run it once a game. Because it would usually only work once, Coach Shaffer would wait to call it at that one point in the game where it would be the most effective. It only worked if the other team was playing a man-to-man defense, which Outlook always did against us, because of our outside shooting. Why it worked is because any Peerless shot that year usually came off of one of three scenarios: A shot or layup coming off the fast break, a shot coming off a screen from our passing game offense, or a shot coming off a pass from dribble penetration. This shot came off a back cut, and it almost always worked because the other team was not expecting it.

On this play, Bill would setup on the low post, weak side. I would be the weak side guard as we ran a two-guard front on offense, Jon and me. Jon would be the strong side guard. Bill would break from the block diagonally up to the high post, center, Jon would pass the ball to him, and then I would make a sharp back cut to the block as Bill was just about to get the ball. I got a half step on my man, and Bill spun and gave me a perfect bounce pass for the layup. We trailed by only one point with less than a minute left!

Outlook was in the bonus, and we didn't want to foul because they were all great free throw shooters. Well, not all of them, but they never let the ones who weren't get the ball! They were in a four-corners set and were going to force us to foul, and then, somehow, one of Outlook's guards made a mistake handling the ball! We got a steal, and Jon and I were slowly bringing the ball up the court with less than 30 seconds left with a chance to take the lead against Outlook! Peerless' first ever State tournament berth was within reach! The crowd was in a frenzy!

But coming down the court on offense, we didn't execute very well and didn't get a good shot off. We were out of timeouts, so Coach Shaffer couldn't call a timeout to setup a play. With about ten or so seconds left, we took a shot, and it wasn't a good shot. Outlook got the rebound, and we fouled. They made both free throws and the game was over. 63–60 was the final.

The Prison Follows Us

It was odd, as I sat there watching Outlook receive the first place trophy. First, what was odd was Flaxville fans *cheered* for Outlook when they received the first place trophy. That was *definitely* odd. Had Outlook lost, Flaxville couldn't challenge because they had lost to them semi-final night. Then, I wondered, what about the third place trophy, and the second place trophy? It seemed something was missing. Then, only moments after having had the prize within our grasp, our first ever trip to State a real possibility and a lifelong dream come true, I started to get the sinking feeling that we had another game to play, and it was against Flaxville, a team that had dominated us for three straight years.

After upsetting Outlook on semi-final night at District, we thought we had finally escaped from District 1-C. But we really hadn't. Now, at Divisional, we had just lost to Outlook in the championship, and Flaxville was waiting in the weeds, eagerly looking forward to their challenge against us on Monday night. So, after two frustrating, disappointing exits from the tourney at District in 1976–77, we were faced yet again with the prospect of being eliminated from the tournament by 1-C teams, this time at Divisional. To make it to State, we would have to escape from District 1-C. Again.

The bus ride home from Wolf Point that night was quiet, deathly quiet. Each player just looked straight ahead, barely ever glancing sideways to talk to the player sitting next to him. I remember my thoughts were along the lines of, "Man, we were close, so close to doing it, to making it to State, had the trophy within our grasp and let it slip through our fingers, and now we have to play Flaxville, yet again."

The Great Intelligence Blunder

On Sunday, the day after we lost the Divisional championship game to Outlook, the greatest intelligence blunder in the history of District 1-C basketball—perhaps even the history of Class C basketball—occurred. In my mind, the drastic consequences it would have for Flaxville on Monday night would be far more severe than the breakdown in intelligence we had at Pearl Harbor in 1941. To this day, the source of this massive intelligence blunder on the part of the Flaxville Cardinals is unknown. I have my suspicions, but our informant, the agent we had working for us, who I *am* going to out, would not reveal *his* source. It was very frustrating that our informant, who was already betraying someone on the other side, could not take it a step further and let us know who his source was. I hate spies with integrity.

Okay, I said I was going to out our informant. His name was Kelly Norman, from Scobey. Now, I know a lot of Peerless kids didn't like him; he could be brash, arrogant, things like that, but your opinions of him might change a little when I reveal the invaluable piece of intelligence he passed to Jon and me the night before we played Flaxville in the challenge game. Jon and I were sitting around the house on Sunday evening, and it was starting to get late. We were wondering if our informant was going to pass us any information at all. Then, just when we had begun to give up hope, the call came. Jon and I leaped for the phone. Normally when Kelly passed us any kind of intel, he would start by talking about the normal stuff, you know, girls, movies, music, that kind of thing. But on this particular night, with the stakes higher than they'd ever been before, we wanted him to cut right to the chase. "Alright Kelly, what do ya got for us?"

"Oh, you're not going to believe this," he said. He had something big for us and we could sense it.

"Okay, Kelly what is it?"

"Well," he said, "seems there is a prediction going around Flaxville that they're going to beat you guys by 20 points tomorrow night. Like it's not even going to be a game. My analysis is, they might be a little over-confident."

Wow! This was big! This was huge! Thanks Kelly! This was a huge intelligence score, and Jon and I couldn't wait to get to school the next day to spread the word.

On Monday morning at school, the intelligence we had collected the previous night from our informant spread through the Peerless battlements like wildfire. "Hey, did you hear what Flaxville thinks of us?"; "Hey, guess how bad they think they're going to beat us, by 20 points," and so on. We were starting to get a little fired up. The last thing you want to do is give your opponent, especially an opponent you have manhandled for the past three years, any kind of incentive to beat you, any kind of combustible fodder to fan the flame. But unfortunately for the Cardinals, they had (unknowingly) done just that, in the most serious intelligence blunder in District 1-C Basketball History. The consequences for the Cardinals on Monday night would be disastrous . . .

Oh, I almost forgot, who was Kelly's source? I have it narrowed down to two people. The first one I think it might have been is Ronnie Dickman, a guy Kelly knew from Whitetail. I thought it could be Ronnie because, although he went to Flaxville High School, he was from Whitetail and maybe had some loose ties with Flaxville because of that. Or maybe he had an axe to grind with them from when he played basketball against Flaxville while he went to elementary school at Whitetail. I don't know. Not only that, Jon and

I had bonded with Dickman when we played against him in fourth grade while he was at Whitetail. In fact, the last game Jon and I played in the old gym at Peerless, in the winter of 1971, was against Ronnie Dickman's team from Whitetail. Our Cougar team went a perfect 9–0 that year, and the game we played against Whitetail in the round robin tournament with Opheim, Whitetail and Peerless was for the championship. Whitetail had beat Opheim, and we had beat Opheim that afternoon. Whitetail was undefeated and Peerless was undefeated. I remember Whitetail even had cheerleaders! Their big cheer was, "We must, we must, we must beat Peerless!" Over and over again! We won 39–25, but the game was far closer than the final score indicated. It was a great game, and we had completed the perfect 9–0 season. After the game, I remember standing against the wall on the entry side of the old gym (there was no room to sit, the gym was packed) talking to Ronnie Dickman about our game and the season as we watched Ed Puckett's girls team, the Hellcats, play their game. The Hellcats were led by Wanda Hames, a tremendous athlete, mother of Adam Morrison, former Gonzaga All-American and current Los Angeles Laker. Anyway, we had gained a lot of respect from Dickman, you know, beating his undefeated Whitetail team like that in this very important fourth grade championship game, and maybe he had carried that with him all those years . . .

But a second, and more likely source, was Connie Lekvold, Kelly's next door neighbor in Scobey. I always thought it might be her because she was dating Cory Tryan, one of Flaxville's starting guards. Since Connie was Kelly's next-door neighbor, I knew he talked to her a lot, and maybe Cory had casually let the prediction slip to her on Sunday night while they were talking at the movies on a date or something. Plus, Connie had blood relatives in Peerless; she was cousins with Marlene Trangsrud and Val Jones, and we all know blood runs thicker than water. Flaxville, betrayed by a woman from Scobey to help Peerless. A very possible scenario. In any event, whether Kelly's source was Ronnie Dickman or Connie Lekvold, the resultant classified information we had collected was all we would ever need to know.

Stay tuned for Monday Night Basketball in Montana!

The Picture Window

Short little segment I remember about my dad, Tiny Puckett, standing beside me as we looked from the picture window of our house, Sunday afternoon before the challenge game against Flaxville Monday night.

I mentioned before that our path to the championship game at Divisional in Wolf Point seemed so swift that we hardly had time to pause and think about where we were: That we were in the championship game at Divisional and right on the edge of our lifelong dream of making it to State. Well, between the time we lost to Outlook Saturday night and played Flaxville Monday night, we had plenty of time to think about it. About 48 hours to be exact. Not only that, because of what had happened the previous two seasons, we had become so fixated on just getting out of our District that a trip to State seemed distant; we hadn't thought about it much because we needed to accomplish the first step before we could even think about the next step. Now we could think about it.

On Sunday afternoon at home, I found myself standing at our picture window next to my dad in our living room, just looking out the picture window at the town of Peerless. I don't remember saying anything to him, or him saying anything to me. We just stood there together, quietly looking out the window, thinking, contemplating. He was on my left. I looked over at him but he didn't look back at me; he just kept looking out the picture window. He had an ever so slight frown on his brow, very slight. Looking out the window, we could see the new gym up the hill to the left; the old gym was just beyond Uncle Reese's house, just a little bit to the left if we were looking straight ahead. I honestly can't remember if I could see the old gym from our picture window or not, but I knew it was there. I know we had to be thinking the same thing: All those cold winter nights going up to play in the old gym with him, to practice and play, Dad teaching us, Jon and me. All the fun we had had, playing basketball together with him coaching us. All the State tournaments we had gone to see with him, since 1975 when Westby won it for the second time, making the annual Holy Basketball Pilgrimage to

Helena, the Mecca of Class C Basketball. At Helena we would watch the other teams play and imagine that someday we would be there, with our team, on that court, playing in the State tournament. And now, after all those years, we had a shot. We were close. One more win and we were going to State. The dream was within reach. Later on that same week, after the game on Monday night, he told me what he was thinking as he we stood there together looking out the picture window that afternoon. After the challenge game against Flaxville, I'll let you know what it was . . .

The Oracle

At home, Dad would often talk for hours about basketball, and longer if you let him. He could go on some rather lengthy orations. One of them I will relate here, as it is especially relevant to the Monday night challenge game at hand. He delivered it to me before I was ever even in high school, still in junior high. I'll recall it as best I can. It won't be exact, but it will be close:

"There are two tournament games you never, ever want to play in. The first one is on Saturday morning, after a tough semi-final loss the night before. You are emotionally and physically exhausted from the game the night before, and the other team is rested, coming from the loser's bracket. You will see a lot of upsets in these Saturday morning games. The second game you never want to play in is a Monday night challenge game at Divisional if you've lost the championship game. In the challenge game, you've had a day to rest, so fatigue is not such a big deal. The big factor is the emotional letdown after the championship game, and there will be no crowd there. The gym will feel like it's empty. Everyone from all the other schools will have gone home. It's a school night, and so it will just be the fans from the two teams at the game, and it will be hard to adjust to that after playing in the packed gym Saturday night. It will be hard to get going. You'll see a lot of upsets in this game, too." Thus spoke Tiny.

I already knew he was right about the Saturday morning games. I had played in two of them already, my freshman and sophomore year at District, both after tough semi-final losses, and both times we were upset by Antelope in the morning and eliminated from the tournament. My freshman year, we had lost to Outlook in the semi-finals and scored 46 points against Antelope in the morning. My second lowest point total in my high school career. My sophomore year, after losing to Westby 72–70 in double overtime semi-final night, we played Antelope the next morning. We had beaten Antelope twice during the season, averaging 75 points in the two games. At District, we scored 41 points, 34 points less than what we had averaged and the lowest point total in my *entire* four-year high school career. *Ever.* It was just awful, it felt like I was just physically beat and emotionally spent but still trying to play. Dad was right again, of course.

Riding Into Battle and a Prediction

Dad's oration about never wanting to play in a Saturday morning or Monday night game was in the back of my mind as we were riding the bus to Wolf Point for the challenge game. I wondered if he would be right again. The previous year, 1977, Flaxville had lost one game all year, and after they lost a tough championship game to Antelope at Divisional, Richey upset them on Monday night in the challenge game.

We were a lot looser on this bus ride than we were on the ride back to Peerless after we lost the championship game. Bernie Wasser and someone else were playing around with a cassette recorder, pretending to be interviewed before the game by an announcer, and then making a recording of it. I couldn't hear what they were saying, just could see they were having a lot of fun. It would be interesting to learn later after the game what Bernie and company had been saying on that tape! Seems Bernie had made a prediction of his own about the outcome of the game on that tape and we shall see how close he was!

A Sluggish Start

When we took the court against Flaxville Monday night, there were more people at the gym than I had expected. The Peerless crowd was there in full force, as was Flaxville's, and I did notice a smattering of fans from teams that had played at Divisional that year, like Richey. Plus, there were a lot of local fans from Wolf Point there, fans we had picked up as the tournament went on because they liked watching our fast paced style of basketball. But the gym was far from capacity, and it was weird, playing in such an important game as this, with a trip at State on the line. But the Peerless and Flaxville fans were loud, and as I looked at Kevin Hatfield jumping against Joel Dighans for the opening tip, the traditional "Go Cards Go!" and "Go Panthers Go!" cheers were echoing through the gym.

The game started out the way every Flaxville-Peerless game had started out in my high school career: Slow, half court, pound it inside for Flaxville, with us only getting one shot on offense on the other end. It was the worst possible scenario for us to start the game. Why couldn't we run against this team? Just couldn't seem to do it, they had our number. Their guards were good and they could handle our press, and they got back on defense. Terry Bakken was a great coach and their team played outstanding defense. It was another frustrating start to a string of frustrating games (seven losses in a row) against Flaxville. At the end of the first quarter, we had a tallied a whopping six points on the scoreboard; Flaxville had 14. The six-point total in the first quarter was the lowest point total for any quarter of any game I played in high school. *Ever.* Dad was right again; "It would be hard to get going."

Dad was right about the crowd too. The Peerless and Flaxville fans were loud, but the eeriest sound you can hear in a game is the sound of the ball bouncing after it goes through the net, and then echoing off the gym wall. When Flaxville would make a basket, you would hear a cheer, but it would seem to fade quickly and then you could hear the ball bounce before you picked it up to inbound it. Bounce . . . bounce . . . bounce. What was that sound?

Bounce... Bounce... Bounce

The second quarter was a little better than the first, but we were still playing Flaxville's game and that was not good. We basically took what they gave us: Stayed in our half court offense, running our passing game offense and looking for a good shot off of it. We got some good screens and some good looks and started to make some baskets. We looked to fast break at every opportunity but there were no opportunities. Another quarter in the half court against Flaxville. At the end of the first half, Flaxville led 24–20. The only other game we had scored fewer points than that in the first half that year was against Outlook at Outlook where we scored 19 points. And the worst part about Flaxville keeping us in the half court was it didn't allow the crowd—our crowd, and the local Wolf Point fans who liked to watch us play—to get into the game.

The third quarter started where the second quarter left off. It felt like we starting the game all over again. They got the tip, came down and scored underneath. We came down, missed a shot. They got the rebound, came back down slowly, executed their offense, and scored underneath again. And you could hear the ball bounce .. . bounce . . . bounce . . . at a very sloooooooow pace as it went through the net. Oh no. Here we go again. This same pattern would repeat itself for two more field goals for Flaxville without a response from us, and suddenly we were down 32–20 in the second half against this powerful Flaxville team, struggling, laboring, looking exactly like the 61–46 loss to them in the District championship. The situation was grim, but not hopeless.

The Caged Panther

We were like a Panther in a cage, a Panther that had been in a cage for seven straight games against this team, and the energy, the pacing back and forth in the cage, was building. I remember a lot from that tourney run; some of it is a little hazy, and some of it is crystal clear. What I'm about to relay next is crystal clear; I can see and hear it in my mind as if it only just happened, is happening now.

Jon and I brought the ball up the court. I was thinking, "The only thing you can do is keep playing, keep executing your offense, don't lose your poise, stay with the team, don't panic, and *let the game come to you.*" We ran our motion offense. I came off a screen set from Bill on the right side of the court, Jon gave me a pass, I calmly took the shot from just to the right of the top of the key. Swish! Jon said, *"Nice shot Joey!"* He had fire in his voice and in his eyes. A *lot* of energy. It was our first basket of the second half, and it picked our crowd up too. In the midst of this dismal game, there was hope. A glimmer. Just don't give up.

Before that shot in the third quarter, I was beginning to wonder if the intelligence we had collected from our informant from Scobey on Sunday night was going to come true. Looked like they *were* going to blow us out. This was a critical point in the game. We could pack up, go home, fold and concede, or gut it up and continue to fight. After that shot, and after that dry spell we had to start the second half, the crowd began to stir, and we started to come to life. This wasn't just the Peerless crowd. It was the Wolf Point crowd too, and some of the fans from the other schools. They had watched us play our up-tempo game in the three previous games against Frazer, Richey and Outlook, averaging 67 points a game, and they were looking forward to watching another round of Peerless style basketball. But they had yet to see it in this game. They had been silent almost this entire game as they watched the taller, slower Flaxville team box us into their half court game and limit us to 20 some points into the third quarter.

As the third quarter progressed, we began to start pressuring the ball a little more, man-to-man pressure full court. Part of the reason we were able to do this was because our shots were beginning to fall, so we could setup our press. It was almost like Jon and I were back in the old gym, shooting on one side of the court with Coach Gene Thompson on the other end, and you knew *you couldn't miss.* We could never get a second shot against Flaxville. Alright. Fine. Then let's *not miss* the first one. We knew if we were going to have a chance, we had to start making shots, break out of the half court into the open court, get turnovers and start to run and shoot. It was

Jon Puckett and Kevin Hatfield battle as Joel Dighans looks on.
Divisional challenge game, 1978. Wolf Point Herald-News photo.

the only way we were going to beat this team. We trailed by 8 to 10 points much of the third quarter, but we made a run at the end of the quarter to pull within four points, 36–32 and we had some momentum, and the crowd was really starting to get into it. But more importantly, the pace of the game had quickened, and the court was beginning to open up. Dad's oration was still true: He only said it would be *hard* to get it going, not that you *couldn't* get it going.

The Cage Opens

As both teams ran out onto the court to start the fourth quarter, the "Go Panthers Go!" and "Go Cards Go!" cheers were a thousand times louder than they had been at the start of the game, louder than they had ever been for any Flaxville – Peerless game. Our crowd was picking us up again. And we were, finally, in the last quarter of the eighth game I'd played against this team in high school, on the edge of breaking out into the open court . . .

The fourth quarter, as best as I can describe it, was a lot like streaks of blue and gold colors lasing across the court, darting quickly from left to right, up and down, every direction, scorching the net with baskets from every angle. The scoreboard was lighting up like a pinball machine. Jump shots, layups, shots of every kind were raining down like artillery fire from all over the court. It was like we had bottled up our open court game against Flaxville for three years, had compressed the intensity of that, and then released it all in one quarter. We traded baskets with Flaxville to start the quarter, and they even expanded their four point lead to six and maybe eight at one point, but it didn't matter: The game had transformed into an open court game, and we were running up and down the court, pressuring the ball, forcing turnovers, shooting pull up jump shots off the fast break. And then Flaxville started to quicken their pace as well and run with us. They couldn't help it, and it was just what we wanted.

To maximize our fast break and scoring potential, Coach Shaffer had inserted Bernie Wasser into the game. We were going with three guards—an all out offensive blitz, kind of like pulling your goalie out

Bernie Wasser shoots a free throw late in Divisional challenge game, 1978.

in hockey and replacing him with another attacker. If Flaxville got the ball past half court, we were dead, but we weren't letting them do that too often; the press was shaking them up. I can't remember when we caught them. I think I remember seeing the score at 44–38 and then we reeled off six straight points to tie it, traded baskets with them a couple times down the court, and then just as soon as we had tied it we took the lead! We had never led the entire game, and then we finally had the lead and it was getting past the midway point of the fourth quarter.

The Dream Comes True

By this time, our crowd, and the Wolf Point fans that had been sitting back waiting for the fireworks to begin, were in a frenzy. Then, just as soon as we had taken the lead, we expanded it to four points, then six! I stole the ball and raced down the left side of the court (where our crowd was), made a layup, and we were up by six points! Bernie Wasser was lighting it up with jump shots from the baseline, and we were all on fire. Ka-ching! Ka-ching! And then, with less than two minutes left, and our lead at about six to eight points, Flaxville started to foul us. Bill Fladager made some key free throws. Jon making a couple free throws, increasing our lead, and then Bernie Wasser was at the line. With about 30 seconds left, Bernie Wasser was at the line and I was at half court with Jon, looking up at the scoreboard in front of me, up on the wall to the left. I looked over at Jon and he looked at me, and the only thing we could do was smile at each other and shake our heads. Unbelievable. We were going to State! The pace of that fourth quarter had been so blistering that we didn't really have time to see the mountain peak as we approached it. It was like all of a sudden we were on top of it, looking down, and we didn't know how we got there. At that point the Peerless crowd, all of them standing, had a sort of going-to-State chant going, but I can't remember what it was.

Then, with the game out of reach, the countdown began: Ten! Nine! Eight! Seven! Six! Five! Four! Three! Two! One! It's over! It's over! Get out of the way! Pandemonium on the court! The Panthers are swarming the court! The Peerless Panthers have done it! For the first time ever in the school's history, the Peerless Panthers are going to State! Lock up the women and children, grab the shotgun and bolt the door because the Peerless Panthers are coming to Helena! Can you believe it! Can you believe it! Oh my goodness!

GAME NOTES . . . final score was 61–52 . . . Peerless made 17 of its last 21 shots from the floor . . . Peerless scored 29 points in the fourth quarter, almost equaling the 32 points scored in the previous three . . . On the bus ride down to the game, Bernie Wasser had predicted Peerless would win by nine points . . . Joe, Jon and Bernie together matched Flaxville's total of 52 points . . . Peerless also scored only six points in the first quarter of its upset of #1 Westby in 1975.

Co-Captains Roger Trang and Bill Fladager accept second place trophy following Divisional challenge game, 1978. Daniels County Leader photo.

The Happy Locker Room

In the locker room after the challenge game against Flaxville, the feeling was a lot different than what it had been after the semi-final upset against Outlook at District. At District, it was a feeling of tremendous relief, the relief of overcoming frustration after two previous years of early exits from District and *finally* getting to Divisional. After the Flaxville game, it was a feeling of not what we had escaped *from*, but where we were going *to*: Helena. State. The Grand Salami. The Big Dance! The dream we'd had since third grade. It was an unbelievable feeling. Can't even begin to describe it.

Jubilant Panthers carry Coach Shaffer off the court following Divisional challenge game, 1978. Wolf Point Herald-News photo.

A lot of people from Peerless came into the locker room to celebrate. It was like a party in the locker room. Coach Shaffer said a few words to the team, and then the team got in a circle and put their hands in the middle, like we did before each quarter or after a timeout, and we all looked at each other and were smiling and waiting for someone to say something profound, or, really life altering, you know, to match the moment, the biggest moment in Peerless basketball history (so far). Then, it seemed like all at once we all started chanting "Go Cards Go! Go Cards Go! Go Cards Go!" with our hands in the middle going up and down. Sorry. Guess this was the best we could do. This might seem like bad sportsmanship, but I don't think it was. We were in our own locker room and weren't doing it in front of the other team, or their fans. I think it was just a release of the frustration of losing to this very good team seven times in a row, for three years in a row; and they were our neighbors in the County so we would see them a lot during the year and it would remind us of their dominance. It was hard to get beat like that again and again and I think we were releasing some built up steam. I mean, it wasn't like we did after the semi-final upset of #1 Westby at District in 1975 when the "Ranger Country" banner was

unceremoniously snipped down at Plentywood Gym, in front of God and everyone! At the tail end of our "Go Cards Go" chant, Cory Tryan, one of Flaxville's fine guards, came into our locker room to shake our hands and congratulate us. This was a great gesture of sportsmanship on Cory's part, and I'll never forget it. This was his last game in high school. His team had lost a tough challenge game to go to State the year before as well, so I'm sure it was very difficult for him to congratulate us as he did.

Joe Puckett takes the nets following Divisional challenge game, 1978.

The Caravan and Homecoming

Then there was the caravan ride home. There was a homecoming reception waiting for us at the Peerless Gym, a microphone set up and everything. The Peerless Gym was almost full at 10:30 PM, and even people that had not made the trip to Wolf Point to see us play came up to the Gym. Marvin Hash, our Superintendent, emceed the ceremony. It was appropriate that he would be the one to do it, as he was the leader of all of us. Coach Shaffer, the coach who all of us liked, the coach whom we had triumphantly carried off the court at Wolf Point, spoke to everyone. Then Marvin Hash called Roger Trang up, one of our co-captains along with Bill Fladager. I was amazed at how poised Roger was talking in front of all those people. He gave a great speech. At the end of Roger's speech, he said, "Someone on the bus ride down said whomever wanted it more would win . . . guess we wanted it more." Roger brought the house down with that one, and I remember Marvin Hash had a big smile on his face. As Roger walked away, Mr. Hash applauded as well.

The Peerless Bar was open for business late on that Monday night and it was hopping. Everyone left the gym to go down to the bar and share in the celebration. A beverage or two was being partaken of by a few of the adult folks there, let's just say. I was sitting there soaking it all up, enjoying the biggest moment of my life, and loving every minute of it. At one point that night in the bar, one man sitting at the bar having a beverage said, "Who the hell do we play anyway, Wibaux? Where the hell is Wibaux?" But late that night, before the ink was dry on the Tuesday morning edition of the Billings Gazette announcing that Peerless had "qualified for the State Class C basketball tourney for the first time in the school's history," people from all over the state of Montana were asking, "Where the hell is Peerless?" Well, they were about to find out . . .

A Prayer from the Heart

I mentioned that I'd tell you what Dad was thinking on that Sunday afternoon before the challenge game as we were looking out the picture window of our house. He told me later that week after the game against Flaxville . He said—and this is an exact quote—"Joey, I prayed on that one." And I remember thinking, "Well that's normal, you know, pray for strength, pray to do your best." But no, that's not what he meant. He prayed about the *outcome* of the game. For Peerless to win. Said he'd never done it before, nor would he do it since. Now, two things: I don't believe that Dad's prayer had anything to do with the outcome of the game, because I think God has more important things to do than affect the outcome of Divisional challenge games. Maybe State championship games but definitely not Divisional challenge games. The second thing is, Dad's heart was in the right place. He knew how much Jon and I wanted to go to State, how much he wanted it, and I think he was really praying for the three of us to do our best and just maybe got a little carried away, you know, caught up in the moment. But I hope this story does tell you just how much Dad wanted the three of us to make it to State.

A Little Levity

Now, since we are going to State for the first time in our school's history, let's celebrate a little and take time out for some comic relief. Here is a joke about just how bad Tiny Puckett wanted to go to State. It relates to the story I just told.

Here's the joke: I never actually asked Dad to Whom he was praying that day. Oh oh, had Tiny Puckett sold his soul to the devil, the Dark Lord of Basketball, for a trip to State?

Dad said, "Joey, I prayed for us to make it to State that day we stood at the picture window."

I said, "Well Dad, that's ok, I know you really wanted all of us to go. It's alright, I'm sure God's not going to hold it against you."

Dad replied, "Well, you're right Joey, God's not going to hold it against me, but someone is."

I couldn't believe it. "What?!!" I said, "You sold your soul to the Dark Lord of Basketball for a trip to State?"

And Dad answered, "No, I already did that. I sold it to beat Outlook so we could get out of District. It was your soul I sold to get to State."

"Dad! You can't sell my soul too! I'm your son, you can't do that!"

He said, "Well let me tell you about the deal, it's not so bad when you hear it."

I said, "Ok, tell me."

He said when he talked to the Dark Lord, the Dark Lord told him that there was no basketball in heaven, no courts, hoops, nothing. Couldn't play basketball in heaven. So the Dark Lord told him, "Wouldn't that be like hell anyway? What do you have to lose? Just be a little hotter here, that's all."

And Dad said he told the Dark Lord, "Ok, now that you put it that way, you're right. You got me. I'm in. Get us out of District and you've got my soul."

So I said, "Well, I guess that's not so bad. Can't play basketball in heaven anyway, and I'll be with you. What about Jon?"

Dad said, "I'm saving his for next year in case we need it." (We would.)

Then I said, "Ok, you, me, and possibly Jon sold out to the Dark Lord of Basketball. What about Mom?"

And then Dad looked at me, smiled, and said, "Joey, what kind of man do you think I am?"

The Magic
that was Helena

Preparing for State

One of the coolest things about the tournament run was we got to play more basketball, a *lot* more basketball—both practice and games—and we got to miss a *lot* of school. Because of the blizzard before District, we played that tournament on Monday, Tuesday and Wednesday. Divisional was the following week, on Thursday, Friday and Saturday, and then we played Monday night against Flaxville. State was the following week, beginning on Thursday, but we left Peerless on Tuesday morning to get there! The night before we left, there was a rousing pep rally held at the gym, followed by a big community pot luck. I can't remember the details of the pep rally, except for the unforgettable, inimitable, unconquerable, SUPER PANTHER! Who was that masked woman with the long flowing cape wreaking havoc on all those opponents on the court? Super Panther had made her debut at the pep rally before Divisional tourney, and I remember I wanted to see more. It was Annabelle Fouhy, and she was brilliant! The pep rally was very creative; a lot of thought went into it, and we were smiling and pretty pumped up after it was over.

On the way down to Helena, we had practice at Northern Montana College in Havre on Tuesday afternoon and then at College of Great Falls on Wednesday. Part of the reason for the practices on the way was most of our team got the flu late in the week after the Flaxville win, and we maybe had one full team practice that entire

75

week. Taking the two days to get to Helena just made the whole experience even more special. We got to take our time, have fun along the way, play basketball, and just enjoy the journey to Helena to play in the State basketball tournament.

Over 125 adult reserved tickets for the tourney were sold in Peerless, and 50 student tickets, plus 20 free passes. We were up to about 200 tickets for Peerless fans before the tourney even started, and, as you will see, we picked up a few more fans at Helena! Peerless alumni from all over Montana, and even other states, descended on Helena to watch us play. I didn't realize at the time that any of this was happening. I was just thinking about playing in the State tournament for the first time and how exciting that was. I had no idea until we ran onto the court to play our first game against Wibaux at 9:00 Thursday night just how many Peerless fans were going to be there, and how loud they were going to be!

A Most Gracious Host

This was the 22nd consecutive year that the State Class C basketball tournament was played in Helena, first at Helena High, then at the Carroll College Physical Education Center, which seated about 4,200 people. This is one of the things that made the experience of playing in that State tournament in 1978 (and 1979) so special. I have to write about this because it is such a big part, a *huge* part, of the story.

Over the course of those 22 years, Helena had really learned to be a fabulous host to the eight teams and their fans that came to the city for the tournament. Everything was well organized. Banquets for the teams were held on Wednesday night, the Helena Independent Record newspaper covered the tournament as its number-one sports story, and two separate Helena radio stations, KCAP 1340 AM and KBLL 1240 AM, called the games. Hotels and restaurants all had "Welcome Class C Tourney Fans" signs up. And, most importantly, the people of Helena *loved* to watch Class C basketball. In short, the Class C basketball tournament was the only show in town that weekend. And you felt, as a player, as you crested the mountain driving from Great Falls to Helena and looked down into the valley of the city of Helena, that the people in that city were waiting for you, that they were expecting you, and that you were going to be very warmly welcomed. This made playing in the State tournament at Helena very, very special. The Helena people had watched those tournaments over the years and had really come to appreciate Class C basketball, how unpredictable it was, how free-flowing it was, and just how plain exciting it could be. I know this because I, along with Jon and several of my teammates, was at several of those 22 consecutive tournaments beginning in 1975 when Dad, Jon and me (and some of our teammates) would make the annual pilgrimage to Helena to watch the tournament.

Helena's Choice

Each year, the Helena fans would pick a team to be their favorite, and would cheer for that team really hard. The team they would pick would usually be an underdog, with a fast-paced style of play, guard-oriented with good outside shooters. In the first round of the tournament, the Helena fans would watch each game, make their assessment, and, sure enough, a favorite would emerge. Some years would be more dramatic than others, but there would always be one team that would stand out to be their favorite. In 1976, the first year Flaxville won the tournament, their favorite team was Box Elder. They were my favorite too! A very exciting team to watch, with a dynamic, electrifying point guard named Gus Bacon.

Who would the Helena fans choose for their favorite in 1978? Hmm . . . let's see, a massive underdog, with a free-flowing style of play and excellent outside shooters . . . who could it be?

The Ultimate Underdog

It's really hard to describe just how much of an underdog Peerless was going into the tournament in 1978. For the Peerless teams that played at State in later years (1982, 1988, and 1995), this was not the case: Peerless was always a respected name coming into State because we had been there before. But in this State tournament, we were the underdog in almost every category. No one picked us to even win a game. We had the smallest school, 34 students (35 counting Superintendent's dog). Superintendent Marvin Hash put that in the program and I hated him for it! Like you want to call attention to that kind of thing! That was just his sense of humor though! At 18–9, we had by far the worst record of any team in the tournament. We had taken fourth in our conference, second at District and second at Divisional. We were the only team of the eight teams that had not been to State before. And last, but certainly not least, we had the smallest team in the tournament. We didn't have a six-footer on the roster. Our "front line" was 5'9", 5'9" and 5'11", with 5'9" and 5'10" in the backcourt. Our sixth man was 5'8". The Independent Record referred to us as the "Cinderella" team in the tournament, and given everything I've just relayed, it would have been a big surprise if they didn't label us that way. So, when we ran onto the court late on Thursday night, the first time in history that a Peerless team had ever taken the court at the State tournament, we had everyone—including perhaps our own Peerless fans—right where we wanted them: No expectation whatsoever.

But it was hard to read all that stuff in the paper about us being such an underdog, the "Cinderella team in tourney"; we weren't used to that. I mean, we were used to being the underdog, like against Flaxville and Outlook, but not like this. We had a lot of pride and we wanted to come out and show this crowd and the state of Montana how we played basketball in Peerless. We were fired up.

Up on the Stage

We were playing a very good Wibaux team. They had won the Southern Divisional against Terry, the #1 ranked team in the state in the final AP poll. Wibaux had been ranked in the top ten all year. They had a great player in Todd Leach, and they didn't start anyone *under* 6'0". Of course, we didn't start anyone *over* 6'0". We were going to start in a zone against them but would look to pressure them on defense whenever we could. Clark Shaffer's strategy for the tourney, as he was quoted as saying in the Independent Record, was to "run whenever we can."

So we were running out onto that revered stage, the Carroll College Physical Education Center, where I'd watched so many games with Dad and Jon. It was an unbelievable feeling. But the warm up was just typical; we were very focused as a team and were looking forward to the challenge against Wibaux. I did have to glance at the crowd though. In the Peerless section, the crowd went up the entire length from the bottom to the top of the gym; I did have to glance to have a look at that! They were buzzing too; many of the alumni were seeing each other for the first time in several years, it was kind of like a reunion. They were talking to each other and eagerly anticipating Peerless' first game ever in the tourney.

The scouting report on Peerless was to keep us in a half court game and play zone defense, taking away our superior quickness and ability to dribble penetrate and shoot off the dribble. Jon and I, and our team in general, all shot better off the dribble. There were two reasons for that. First, remember the best of seven one-on-one games Jon and I would play against each other? Each game of the series was up to 60 by ones. When Jon and I played these games, the ball would start at the top of the key. Since we both could hit that shot, neither one of us would let the other one just shoot that shot; we pressured the ball and forced a dribble. Then, we would overplay one way or the other on defense, forcing the dribble to the right or left. For some reason, I would usually force Jon to dribble to his right, and Jon would force me to dribble to my left. Because we could each slide our feet pretty well on defense, the dribbler couldn't make it in for a layup. Each of us would usually shoot the pull up jump shot off the dribble, Jon to his right and me to my left. The second reason our team shot well off the dribble was because we practiced it a *lot*. During practice, one of the drills Coach Shaffer would have us do would be to dribble up and shoot off the dribble and both sides of the court, over and over again.

The Magic Begins

So, not surprisingly, Wibaux came out in a zone, and we would have to hit some long-range shots to pull them out of it. They were tall and had long arms and extended their zone pretty far out on the perimeter, so we had to shoot farther out than we normally did against other zones we'd seen that year. I remember in the first half Jon took a shot from a place I had never seen him shoot before—I mean it was *way* out there—and he nailed it. And then he did it again. And with each successive shot our team made over that zone, the crowd started to buzz and really get behind us, and then it was decided: Peerless would be the team in 1978 that the Helena fans would root for! We had the fans early in the first half, and they just kept getting louder and louder as the game went on. Incredibly, as the game unfolded—you couldn't script it any better—we began to play Peerless style basketball like we had never played it before, on that stage, at State, in front of that packed PE Center in Helena. The Helena fans, who had read the paper earlier that day about our nine losses and our lack of a six-footer, did not know what to expect from our team. In the State tourney program, because of a mistake, our names were not even listed under our team picture, and so the crowd could not put a name on any Peerless player before the game started. But early in the first half, when it became readily apparent that our team could play basketball, *really* play basketball, the crowd began to put names to faces rather quickly, and we became the darlings of the tournament, like no team before us at Helena had ever done, and (I would venture to say) no team has done since. It was unbelievable . . .

We led 21–15 after the first quarter and 29–27 at half. Even though we were hitting our shots in the first half, Wibaux stayed in their zone; they didn't want to come out and play us man-to-man because we were so much quicker. So this was a half court game we were playing against Wibaux, a game we didn't like to play, and we really wanted to break it out and open that court up, get out and run and show the fans how we played basketball in Peerless. And in the second half, midway through the third quarter, that court would open up and we would break it open and light it up like never before. And the crowd would go absolutely bananas!

Joe Puckett shoots against Wibaux, State tourney, 1978.
Helena Independent Record photo by Bill Bowman.

Oh Snap!

Wibaux took the lead briefly, 33–31, early in the third quarter, but I remember that the pace of the game had quickened, just like at the end of the third quarter against Flaxville at Divisional. We were pressing full court to force the play, get some turnovers and get into a running game, but then still fall back into our zone if they broke the press. Then, it happened: A point came in that third quarter where the flow of the game suddenly transitioned from a half court game—us shooting shots over that zone—into a wide open, full court, fast breaking, run dribble pass and shoot game, and it seemed to happen with the snap of someone's finger! And then it was open season for the Peerless Panthers in the Carroll College PE Center on a Thursday night! We began to fast break, run and shoot, just like we had done in earlier tournament games, except this time we were doing it at State, in front of fans that had never seen us play before. We were shooting a scorching percentage from the field. Cato "the Cat" Butler, KCAP radio announcer, said on the radio that Peerless needed "asbestos nets" for this game. We were lighting it up from all angles, up and down the floor, dazzling the crowd. The PA announcer in the PE Center began to draw our names out really loud and enthusiastic after every basket a Panther made, like "JOOOOOONNNNNNNNN PUCKETTTTTTTT!!!!!!!!!", "JOOOOEEELLLLLLL DIGHANSSSSSSS!!!!!!!!!!!!", "RO-GERRRR TRRAAAANGGGGGG!!!!!!!!!" "BILLLLLLLLL FLADAGERRRRRRR!!!!" It was like he was our home court announcer! At the end of the third quarter we led 47–40, and we had the momentum and the crowd totally behind us as we vaulted into the fourth quarter.

We didn't even want to go to the bench after the third quarter buzzer went off, just wanted to stay on the court instead and keep playing. In the fourth quarter, we just picked up where we left off in the third, running up and down the court, playing our fast break game. Somewhere in there, Jon had picked up his fourth foul, but Coach Shaffer kept him in the game because it was late in the second half and Jon was hot, I mean hot like I'd never seen him before. Coach Shaffer didn't want to take him out of the game in case he'd get out of the flow and cool off. We just kept running and running and we got our confidence and I remember at a certain point in the game it was just like we were back in Peerless, scrimmaging on a school night with each other in the fall in the gym, running up and down the court having fun, shooting shots from wherever and having a blast playing basketball. It was pure *Joy*. We expanded our lead to 17 points late in the fourth quarter, going on a 38–19 run after Wibaux took the lead early in the third quarter. The crowd was on fire. It was one thing to make it to State, but to play like this on that stage, well . . . no words to describe it! What an experience!

Jon fouled out with about four minutes left in the fourth quarter. He made 10 of 16 shots from the floor that night, most of them long-range bombs. He had played magnificently, and the crowd began to clap as he walked off the court. And then they all stood up and applauded; The Helena crowd gave Jon a standing ovation! I couldn't believe it! It was a great moment for Jon, but now that I look back on it, it was a great moment for all of us, for Peerless basketball. Jon was just one player, but he symbolized what our team was all about, how we played, our spirit: A combination of tremendous hustle, heart, and razor sharp basketball skills. And I know those fans were standing and clapping and cheering not just for Jon, but for Peerless basketball, for a team that had dazzled them with Class C basketball that had not been seen on that court in 22 years. Those fans were clapping for Peerless; for all of us.

GAME NOTES . . . Final score was 69–58 . . . Peerless shot 29 of 48 from the floor . . . We outrebounded the taller Wibaux team 33 to 30 . . . My Uncle Ed Puckett, back home in Peerless, recorded the game on tape while he sat at his kitchen table. He never said a word the entire game, but when the score was 69–52 late in the fourth quarter, he incredulously exclaimed to his wife, Aunt Norma, "They beat the hell of out 'em!"

Cinderella Exposed

On semi-final night we played Manhattan Christian. They were a very, very good team. Number one seed from the West, they had lost only two games all year. They were all over 6'0 tall and had good guard play. No weaknesses, really. They had a great frontline, and were also very well coached. Their coach was Bob Korthuis. He'd been there many years and was very experienced. Jon and I had seen some of his previous teams play in the State tourney when we went there with Dad, and he always put a solid team on the court. In the semi-final game in 1975, Antelope beat a very good Manhattan Christian team. Against us, Christian would come out in an extended 1–3-1 zone and *stay* in that zone no matter how many shots we popped over the top of it. Coach Korthuis had seen enough the previous night against Wibaux when Wibaux switched to man-to-man in the third quarter, and he was not about to make the same mistake and get in a running game with Peerless. Nor would Wibaux make the same mistake against us when we played them in the consolation game the next night. Coach Korthuis also saw very clearly that we shot better off the dribble, and he was going to force us to shoot standing still on the perimeter, stating before the game that he felt Peerless did their best shooting "on the move." So we had been discovered. One of the advantages of being quarantined in District 1-C, as we had been for the previous two years, was that no one in the state had seen us play before; we were able to surprise a lot of people that first night, especially Wibaux. But people were catching on fairly quickly . . .

The Carroll College PE Center was packed that night, and the Helena and Peerless crowd were anticipating another run by the Panthers. We came out of the gate hot, shooting long-range shots over that zone, hitting 6 of our first 8 shots. The crowd was on fire, but we couldn't sustain it; the crowd on this night would not see another Panther upset at State. Christian's 1–3-1 zone really was difficult to master, and they had fairly good guard play so it was difficult for us to press them, although we did force 19 turnovers. We had some flashes and spurts in that game where we displayed the

Joel Dighans shoots against Manhattan Christian, State semi-final, 1978.
Helena Independent Record photo by Bill Bowman.

Peerless brand of basketball. We shot well, and I was amazed at how the crowd stayed with us, *really* stayed with us, even when it got late in the game and it was a rout by Christian. But in the end, their frontline was just too much for us. The final score ended up 75–56, but we were only behind by 5 points at halftime and by 11 at the end of the third quarter; it was only late in the fourth quarter when they were breaking our press and getting easy baskets that made the final score what it was.

So then it was time to go to the hotel, get some sleep and come back to play Brady the next morning. Brady was the #1 seed from the North and top-ranked team in the state for much of the year, as well as the pre-tourney favorite to win it all. Was the magical tournament run of 1978 for the Panthers and their fans about to come to an end? Had the run stopped there against Brady on that Saturday morning, it still would have been the most memorable tourney run of my life, but incredibly, as much fun and excitement as we had had so far in the tournament, the best—the absolute pièce de résistance—was still to come . . .

Saturday Morning

Brady was led by Kevin Kauk, an All-State guard his junior and senior year; and one of the best players in the state. They had a good center, 6'3" Lin Soholt, and were a solid team all around. Jon and I had watched them play the previous year when they played at State. They took third place the previous year. Many of those players had now returned for their senior year; they were experienced—and good.

Now normally, as Dad had orated, playing on a Saturday morning after a semi-final loss was not a game you wanted to play, but this was different. We were at State, and no one had expected us to go this far, so we were looking forward to running out onto that court and playing another game Saturday morning. Plus, Dad always said that it was hard to play on Saturday morning after a *tough* semi-final loss, but we weren't emotionally down after losing to Christian; it wasn't like they beat us on a last second shot. So we were ready to play, both emotionally and physically, on Saturday morning. It was different for Terry, the team Outlook had beat 53–52 in a *tough* semi-final game the night before; they were demolished by Wibaux 64–42 in the first game that morning, so Dad's prophesy played out perfectly in that one.

One of the things I was worried about was the crowd: Would they come back to watch us play on Saturday morning and cheer us on after we had lost to Christian? Well, not to worry! Our Peerless crowd was there in full force, and so were the Helena people! Once the tourney favorite at Helena always the tourney favorite. They had come back to watch us play again on Saturday morning. The gym was at near capacity for those Saturday morning games, and the crowd, again a big factor during our entire tournament run, would once again play to our advantage in this game.

I was a little worried playing this highly touted Brady team; maybe we had only caught Wibaux off guard, and then Christian had caught on and now Cinderella would be exposed before the clock even struck midnight. Maybe we were just an average team that had pulled off a major upset, but now everyone knew us and that would be that. But we would soon learn, as we took the court against Brady, that we belonged on that court with any team in the State, Brady included.

This game would be close all the way, and Brady would lead it most of the time, except in the fourth quarter. The first half, as was typical of many of our tournament games that year (with the exception of Outlook in the second quarter at District), was not the half that we would force the play and press and get out and run. At the end of the first quarter Brady led 21–18, and then they led 30–26 at halftime. We were playing well as a team, but a little sluggish. As always, we wanted to come out in the second half and force the play, get up and down the court into our running game, get the crowd into it. And we did! The crowd came to life in that second half when we came out in the third quarter and started lighting it up again! It wasn't nearly like it was against Wibaux, but we were putting on quite a show again. And at the end of the third quarter, we had closed the gap to 46–44.

Another Upset

When we came out for the fourth quarter, the "Go Panthers Go!" cheer was louder than I'd ever heard it before. Why was that? Well, what was so unusual about it was that the Helena fans were now *joining in* with the Peerless fans as our cheerleaders; Darla Drummond, Val Jones, Barbie Trang, Judy Fouhy and Dannette Dighans led the cheer. It was like the entire Carroll College PE Center was rocking with that cheer! It really picked us up, and no doubt it helped us pull off the upset against Brady that morning.

The game was very close all the way until late, but we finally took the lead at 48–47 in the fourth quarter. Then, it was like that feeling you get that I described earlier: You start to smell the upset, taste it, and then you take your game up another level. That happened again with Brady. We were leading late with a little over a minute left. We were in a four-corners set but Roger Trang went ahead and took a long jump shot anyway (why not?) and nailed it. We had a 58–54 lead! Then, we went into a four corners (for real this time) to force them to come out to foul us; Jon made four free throws down the stretch to seal the win. With each free throw that went in and increased our lead, the Peerless crowd would erupt. And with time running down, I realized we were going to be playing on Saturday night in Helena, for the consolation game against Wibaux. I couldn't believe it! And that consolation game against Wibaux, after everything our team had experienced on that tourney ride so far, would prove to be far more than a "consolation" for us; we weren't exactly "hurting" that bad.

The Best Saturday Afternoon Ever

After the game against Brady, a lot of our fans stayed and waited for us to come out of the locker room. They gave us a tunnel to run through as a team when we exited the gym. Then we went back to the hotel. Talk about a wonderful day. We had just beaten the team that most people had picked to win the tournament, and we had a few hours to relax and hang out and get ready to play on Saturday

Joel Dighans fights for a rebound with Lin Soholt of Brady, State 1978.
Helena Independent Record photo by Bill Bowman.

night! We had a little time to catch our breath, and it was awesome. Now, no matter what the outcome against Wibaux, we knew that we had made our mark on the tourney. People knew the Panthers could play basketball. But if anyone at that point had told us the experience that waited for us Saturday night against Wibaux, we never would have believed them . . .

Saturday Night Live

Playing on Saturday night in Helena! It doesn't get any better than that! The Carroll College PE Center was so crowded that night, it was standing room only; they had to turn people away at the door. This might have been one of the reasons they moved the tourney from Helena, because the Center only seated 4,200 people. But there was nothing like playing in that gymnasium with a packed crowd! Adding to the excitement was Wibaux's outstanding band, who during warm ups played a rousing rendition of "We Will Rock You" and "We are the Champions" from Queen's *News of the World* album. It was amazing that Wibaux's band had mastered these songs since *News of the World* had only been released five months earlier. Their music really got you rocking. Tell me these songs don't get you fired up when you hear them! Our Peerless fans were so pumped up that during warm ups they were cheering louder than I'd heard them at the *end* of some our games!

It was very special warming up on that court that night; we had gained a lot of respect over those three games. But now that we had come this far, we didn't want to make a good showing and call it good. We were playing for the third-place trophy at State, and we wanted it.

Double Jeopardy

One thing that was on my mind, as I ran out onto that hallowed court to play Wibaux again on Saturday night, was previous State C tournaments where a team had won the first game of the tournament, and then had to play them again in the consolation game. This had happened in both 1973 and 1974, and the results were not favorable for the team that had won the first game. In 1973, Randy Selvig's senior year, his Outlook team lost their first game of the tournament to Twin Bridges by 40 points, 82–42. Then, only two nights later, Outlook played that same Twin Bridges team in the consolation game and *beat* them 55–54! The following year, in 1974, Frazer defeated Twin Bridges 75–64 in the first game of the tournament, and then, just two nights later, Twin Bridges defeated Frazer 110–72 in the consolation, setting the single game-scoring record in the history of the Class C tournament!

So, it was not going to be easy beating this excellent Wibaux team a second time—I had no illusion that it was going to be anything but a dogfight playing them again. And it would be . . .

The Longhorn's Learn

Wibaux came out in their extended 1–3-1 zone just like Christian did the night before, and they were *not* going to come out of it to save their lives. I remember those long arms and legs dangling all over the half court like a web; they were pushing us out even further to shoot than in the first game, and they were not about to let us get out and run. I think they were actually playing their point guard back as a free safety! So this was going to be a half court game and we were going to have to take what Wibaux gave us. Joel Dighans, our sophomore center, was going to have to step up in the middle and provide us some inside scoring punch, and he did! Man, did he! He played an absolutely brilliant game, both offensively and defensively, and he was a big reason we were able to stay in the game against Wibaux in the first half. Joel was always a strong center for us inside, but in this game he was extraordinarily good, right when we needed him to really step up.

In fact, all of our wins in that tourney run in 1978 (and later in 1979) were total team efforts, and in every game one player or another would step up and contribute in ways they had never done before. In this game, in the consolation, it just happened to be Joel Dighans. In the challenge game against Flaxville at Divisional, it was

Joel Dighans jumps against Todd Leach of Wibaux, State consolation, 1978.

Bernie Wasser. Roger Trang and Bill Fladager always played steady at forward, and both were tremendous rebounders and passers. Roger was also a great outside jump shooter, and both Bill and Roger were great jumpers. Each played way over their height of 5'9". They were also our co-captains and our leaders. In this game against Wibaux, Ray Chapman would come in the game late in the fourth quarter and hit some key free throws, also helping us to win. Total team efforts, all of them. And players that played tough every day in practice—great team players who would contribute enormously whenever they got the chance in a game—were Willard Fladager, Marty and Perry Thieven, Rick Wasser and Kelly Trang. Dwane Dighans was our manager, a freshman (Coach Shaffer called him "the greenhorn") who would develop and become a great player for Peerless on the 1982 State Team.

As I mentioned, it was not easy playing the same team a second time. Wibaux had learned in that first game how to handle us, and the first half seemed sluggish, slow. We were struggling to get good shots off; I was a little tired, but Joel Dighans and Jon Puckett were keeping us in the game with their shooting. Wibaux was beating us soundly. They led 20–12 at the end of the first quarter and 32–22 at halftime. It really felt like a Flaxville game, one of those games where they just corral you offensively and you can't stop them defensively on the inside, but just lumber up and down the court in slow motion. If we were going to go out with a bang at State, we were going to have to come out strong in the second half, pick up the pace a little, and start making some shots.

The Comeback

And, as if it was scripted, we came out in the second half and did just that. We got the tip, and Roger Trang came down and hit a jumper off the dribble. The crowd stood up and I don't think sat down the rest of the game. The comeback was on!

We gradually began to crawl back into the game in the third quarter. It was hard because it was a half court game, and just like against Flaxville, we had to make sure we got a good shot off because we would probably only get one shot. Jon was shooting phenomenally from the outside, just like in the first game against Wibaux, and Joel was playing tough inside. Late in the third quarter we had cut the lead to 41–36, then I made a wild shot at the buzzer at the end of the third quarter, and another one to start the fourth off the tip, and we had pulled to within one point at 41–40. The crowd was going insane! I can't even describe how crazy the crowd was at that point. The game went back and forth after that, trading baskets with half court possessions, and some free throws. We never took the lead, and were only able to tie it late in the fourth quarter. Ray Chapman made a couple key pressure-packed free throws late in the game to keep us close, and then, with about two minutes left, I made a free throw to tie the score at 49. I missed the second free throw, and Wibaux's Todd Leach came down and scored on a turnaround jumper. Wibaux was ahead 51–49. Then Jon came back down the other end and launched a 30-footer. Swish! Back tied at 51. Then Wibaux came down the court and turned the ball over! We had the ball with a 1:23 left in the game with the score tied! Clark Shaffer called a timeout and with 1:23 left in the game, we went into the huddle to talk it over.

The Grand Finale

In the huddle, Coach Shaffer told us we were going to go into our four corners offense and play for the last shot of the game. We were either going to win it or go into overtime. I wrote earlier that we would usually go for the last shot of any quarter, once the clock got under a minute, so this wasn't anything unusual for us. Coach Shaffer wanted to see if they were going to come out in a man-to-man to pressure the ball or stay back in that zone. Well, not surprisingly, they stayed back in that zone. They weren't about to come out and challenge the ball; they were not going to allow us to beat them off the dribble. Jon and I had the ball out front, weaving back and forth and dribbling the clock down, and passing to the forwards occasionally that would pop it back out. The clock was winding down second by second. The crowd's intensity and expectation was building as each second clicked off the clock. They knew we were going for the last shot and it was going to come down to the wire. Then, with about 12 seconds left, Jon dribbled and let fly a jumper. Swish! The crowd erupted as never before! But wait! Someone on Peerless had called a timeout! What? The shot would not count! What is going on down there on the court! Turned out, Jon was just getting himself (and the crowd) warmed up!

There was about ten seconds left when the timeout was called. In the play Coach Shaffer called in the huddle, I was to inbound the ball, and Jon was the first option off the dribble; I was the second option off a screen winding around on the low post, and Joel Dighans was the third option in the middle. I couldn't believe how cool Coach Shaffer was in the huddle. He said, "Joe, you're a guard!" And then, pausing just for a moment, he realized how silly it was to say that (of course I was a guard!) He smiled at me and said, "Did you know that?" That was how cool Coach Shaffer was. In the middle of that huddle in that crazy situation he was cool, and (as he had done all year) he kept us cool as well.

Jon was hot, and so the ball was going to get in his hands first, and I was going to inbound it. "Go Panthers Go!" was *rocking* through the Center when we ran back onto the court. So here we go! I get the ball to inbound on the left side of the court as we faced the basket. Jon breaks off a screen to get open. I throw it to him and he immediately takes the ball hard on the dribble *to his right* for a few dribbles and picks the ball up, doesn't even set, pivots in the air toward the basket and lets fly with a 20-footer just to the right of the key just like he did against me a thousand times playing one on one in the Peerless Gym. I was running under the basket to come off the screen on the other side of the court, and I saw the ball arcing right toward the basket. I could see the ball was deadly aimed and headed straight for the bottom of the net. I was thinking, "I'm not going to come off this screen, let alone take the shot," and, "Jon, why did you shoot it so soon?" And then: Swish! KABOOM! Timeout Wibaux! Four seconds left! After the timeout, the Panthers mob Jon Puckett on the court. But wait! There are four seconds left! A lot of time left to play in this game!

Panthers leaving the court after winning State consolation game, 1978.

In the huddle, Coach Shaffer told us to play defense at half court, match up with whomever came our way, and don't stay back in the zone, don't let them take the initiative and force the play. Jon was to put pressure on the guy taking the ball out so he couldn't toss it uncontested down the full court to their big center. It was time to come back onto the court for the final four seconds.

The ball is inbounded down the left side of the court coming at us; it's Rod Barnaby coming at me at half court on the dribble, and I can see in his eyes that he's going to let fly with a shot off the dribble at half court. I'm not going to let him do it, though, because I remember Steve Miner's shot in Wolf Point in 1975. I know that shot can be made and I'm not going to let this happen to us, not at State. I see I have a clean block because he has to shoot it from his hip to get enough strength on it so I just put my arms up. I block it! It's cleanly blocked! The buzzer sounds! The game is over! The game is over!

The Peerless Panthers, the underdog of underdogs, have just

captured the third-place trophy at State! The Panthers are mobbing each other on the court! The Peerless fans are jubilant and jumping up and down in the aisles! The greatest moment in Peerless basketball history has just been made! In their first ever trip to the State tournament, the Peerless Panthers, pulling off three major upsets, have captured the third place trophy and will be standing on the podium! Can you believe it! What a finish!

GAME NOTES . . . Jon Puckett and Joel Dighans combined for 36 points for Peerless . . . Peerless outscored Wibaux 31–19 in the second half . . . Outlook, a team we had beaten twice before, would go on to defeat Manhattan Christian 55–51 in the championship game, the fourth time in seven years a 1-C team had won State. . . Joe and Jon Puckett turned 17 years old on that day, March 11, 1978 (Best Birthday I ever had! ya think?) . . . Final record for the Panthers that year was 21–10 . . . On Monday, the AP announced that Jon Puckett from Peerless was voted MVP of the tournament. . . A fairytale end to a fairytale season . . .

Bill Fladager and Roger Trang receive third place trophy.

To the Victors

After Outlook beat Christian in the championship game, it was time for the trophy presentations. After the third place trophy was announced, the crowd erupted as Bill Fladager and Roger Trang, our co-captains, went up to receive it. What a great moment for Roger and Bill, and what a great moment for Peerless basketball. The work (play) was done, and now it was time to just relax and enjoy the experience. And what an incredible experience that was for all of us at State that year. It was really too much to absorb at the time; it took weeks, even months, to come down from it. And I do remember thinking, as I was watching Roger and Bill receive the trophy, "Wow, I am a junior, and I have another year left to play, and isn't it going to be special to come back here to Helena next year to play again in this wonderful tournament." Already, the seed of expectation for a return trip to Helena the following season was germinating As I left the Center that night, after the trophy presentation, a player from Rudyard said, "See you back here next year, Joe!" I didn't realize at the time just how difficult that was going to be, and how utterly and completely different the experience was going to be one year hence . . .

Dave Selvig, Randy Wangerin and Jerry West receive Outlook's first place trophy.

More on how dominant 1-C was back then. Six of the ten players on the all-tourney team that year came from 1-C: Jon and Joe Puckett and Joel Dighans from Peerless, and Randy Wangerin, Jerry West and Dave Selvig from Outlook. It was the sixth time in the 1970's the MVP at State had come from 1-C: Robin Selvig in 1970, Neil Peterson from Westby in 1972, Randy Selvig in 1973, Alan Nielsen from Westby in 1975, Kevin Hatfield from Flaxville in 1976, and then Jon Puckett in 1978. It would be more of the same in 1979 (Kevin Hatfield) and 1980 (Doug Selvig). That same year, in 1978, Craig Guenther, from Antelope, won the MVP in State Class B after Plentywood won the championship; he had transferred to Plentywood from Antelope that year. Glendive won the Class A tourney in 1978, so it was a clean sweep for the East.

Another Perspective

In the aftermath of the State Class C tourney in 1978, the following Letter to the Editor of the Helena Independent Record was sent by Sharon Willey Wosepka from Wibaux. It would contribute, perhaps, to the eventual migration of the State Class C tourney from Helena to a parade of other cities in the state. This letter is emotional, and at times intense, and it reveals just how much the Helena fans rooted for Peerless at State that year. Yes, it's true: Manhattan Christian was booed when they took the floor against Outlook for the championship game because they had beaten Peerless semi-final night. How dare they beat those Panthers!

"Didn't Like the Class C Crowd," Helena Independent Record, March 1978, from Sharon Willey Wosepka

Dear Editor,

Having just returned from a visit to my hometown of Helena for the Class C Tournament, I have spent a few days reflecting on the events of the past weekend, and feel some comments must be made.

I find myself seriously questioning the wisdom of leaving "Class C State" in our capitol. My reasons are:

I doubt, or at least wonder, if Helena's Class C fans realize just how hard it is for a "C" school to make it to State? Do they know there are ninety-six Class C schools in the state, that those teams must make it through not one, but two tournaments, and finish in one of the two top places in order to earn that trip?

Do you Class C fans realize that four of the teams in that tournament traveled a one-way distance of almost 500 miles, with their following, to attend the tournament?

I don't think that Helena fans even begin to fathom what a thrill it is for those boys and their followers to make it to State and what a lonesome feeling it is when 4,000 people are on their feet yelling against you!

I wonder if you realized that there were eight teams in that tournament—not just one?

Wibaux happened to be in the position of playing Peerless—not once—but twice. We were disliked by the crowd for this reason, I suppose, although we certainly have a good team with some outstanding players. But we never received any acknowledgement—listening to Cato (the Cat) Butler, you'd never have known we were on the floor! Our community raised $700 to send our band—a band the whole community is extremely proud of. That band performed for every school we played, yet no kind words or applause were heard from announcer, crowd, paper, or radio. Had we beaten Peerless Saturday night, God knows if our contingent would have made it out of the gym alive. But the final straw—the thing I could not believe—was when Manhattan Christian came out on the floor to warm up for the Championship game, and were booed—booed because they had the audacity to beat Peerless Friday night.

Point of this rhetoric: When the gym is 50 percent full of Helena fans and they must "adopt" a team to the point of complete favoritism and emotionalism (and don't kid yourselves people, the refs can feel the pressure too) then the time has come for a change.

Proposal: Since nearly half of Montana lies east of Billings (does that surprise you?) let's alternate East/West with the 'A' tournament—Metra one year, Carroll the next. This would serve two purposes: 1) cut the driving of the two eastern divisions one out of every two years and 2) perhaps awaken a spirit of appreciation for all eight teams in the fans of Helena. Hosting the State Class C Tournament is not an honor Helena earns, it's a responsibility they ask for.

This is not an empty proposal. There is a movement afoot to do just this with contacts to the MHSA and to Congressman Marlenee. A change is definitely needed in order to insure that Class C State Tournaments remain the finest in Montana.

Billy Beer

Following the consolation game against Wibaux on Saturday, the town of Helena was a rather festive place for people from Peerless. It had been quite a three days! I remember going into a room at the Campbell Lodge Hotel. There were a lot of *extremely* happy Peerless People there! It was a huge party and was probably the most festive room I can ever remember being in. When we left the hotel, Jon and I needed a ride back somehow to the other hotel we were staying at.

There were a lot of kids "out on the town" that night. So, who do we hitch a ride back to our hotel with? Some kids from Wibaux!! "Hey, you guys need a ride? Oh look, it's the Puckett twins! Come on in!" I wasn't so sure about that. You know, like we might drive off a cliff or something. I remember one of the girls in the front seat said very sarcastically after we got in the car, "Ooooo, wow, wait 'till I tell everyone in Wibaux I got to give the Puckett twins a ride in my car!" But they were very friendly and we talked a lot on the way, and it was a nice ride.

Back at the hotel, I remember Coach Shaffer stopped by with Donna Fladager to see us. When he looked at us, he had that smile on his face like "Ok guys, I know you're going to have fun, just don't do anything stupid." I remember Karen Fladager was there too, Bill Fladager's sister; she stopped by our room to talk to Bill, whom Jon and I were rooming with, along with Roger Trang. Now, this was the year 1978, Jimmy Carter was president and he had a brother named Billy. Billy Carter liked to enjoy a beer or two now and again. He was an embarrassment to President Carter because I think he was caught once urinating in public after he got drunk. Well, Falls City Brewing Company started a brand of beer called "Billy Beer" that Billy Carter endorsed and promoted. So, on my birthday in 1978, at my hotel room with Bill Fladager, in celebration of our magnificent tourney run, and in the named honor of one of my team captains, I tipped a Billy Beer with Billy Fladager. This would be the first, last, and only time I would drink a Billy Beer.

Back at the Ranch

When we got back to Peerless from Helena, there were a lot of letters of congratulations sent to the Peerless Panthers, from all over the state, from Peerless alumni, coaches, and others. We also received some letters sent directly to the Puckett house. One letter my dad received came from Mr. Howard Retz, the owner of Retz Funeral Home in Helena. Mr. Retz remembered Dad from 1939 when the Peerless Pirates played in an invitational tournament there. Mr. Retz wrote, "If memory serves me right, you fellows stayed in the old Grand Hotel, since burned down, and you won a hamburger for traveling the greatest distance to the tournament. I was sorry to see you eliminated from that tournament. Will never forget the rebounding done by brother Reese."

Guess those marauding Pirates had been there before the Panthers!

Mr. Retz' letter ended with this: "All Helena is looking forward to your return next year." Thought that was a funny line, especially coming from a mortician. Didn't realize at the time just how much "fun" it was going to be returning to Helena the next year. The road would not be easy . . .

Alpha Twin

Now, here is one more thing about the 1978 tournament regarding my twin brother Jon. It may have appeared to many people who did not know us that we were two indistinguishable twins running around out there on the court, but the fact is we had many differences that had been in place since we were very young, and so here they are.

As I wrote earlier, Jon and I would play one on one series, sometimes up to the best of seven games across several days, each game up to 60 by ones. These series would be very competitive, but the end result would almost always be the same: I would win the series. Jon, I think, maybe won a handful of those series, and we probably played well over a hundred of them. In one of those series, Jon led three games to one and was leading big in the fifth game and I came back to win that game and the series. He picked the ball up after I won the series and threw it as hard as he could at the wall in the new gym out of frustration and then stormed out of the gym.

I also ran up a 33 game win streak against him in "Kleenex Ball", a game we would play at home where we would rap masking tape around a bunch of Kleenex to make a ball, and then cut the bottom out of the Kleenex box and tape it to the wall to make a basket. I posted the number of games I had in the 33 game win streak on the wall after each win. He broke the streak on a fluke shot.

Point of this is that I was severely more competitive than Jon. In baseball, when a big game was on the line, Dad would always hand me the ball to pitch. In basketball, Dad would always have me guard the tougher opponent; expect me to have the "big" game. It would always be me. If you were to look at our statistics in high school, you would always see me averaging about 5–7 more points per game than Jon. I was more aggressive and far more assertive on the court. I started as a freshman in High School, Jon did not. And so on . . .

A Messy Story

Now, just so you don't have to take my word for it, let me allow my friend (and master storyteller) Willard Fladager (PHS '78) to relate a messy story to you about how I refused to let Jon beat me in a cross country qualifying race, despite the powerful urge I had to stop and let him pass me.

It was the usual fall afternoon in Peerless, with a slight breeze coming out of the west (30 mph) with the temp hovering around the 78 (get it) degree range. In the locker room, the members of Peerless first cross country team were getting dressed to go out and do their timed trials. I never liked cross country, never was sure why I did it, just a glutton for punishment I guess. Most of us were getting dressed, but one of our teammates was in the sit-down stall, not having a good start to his timed trials, and we were all wishing that he would have saved it for later or had gone outside (little did we know that we would get one of those wishes, or should I say both at the same time).

Considering the fact that I believe it was our first year or maybe second, we had a very good cross country team. We had already turned into contenders thanks to the likes of Bernie, Joe, Jon, Joel and Ray, and I was just a tag-along. The top 5 runners had a gauge of how slowly a person could make it around the 3.2 mile run. Brian Bechtold started the whole thing as a way to stay in shape for basketball, since we didn't have football. If I remember right, the State Cross Country meet was held in Helena, where we ran the Bill Roberts golf course. Now, when I play there, my memories are much better than that day I had to run the course without any little white ball to chase. I'm a better golfer than I was a runner (which ain't saying much). I think we lost to Frazer, and I believe Bernie was second as well, or maybe he won it that year.

Anyway, back to the timed trials. The stall was emanating some odiferous odors, not as bad as Jack's in Saco, but damn close. Needless to say, we were all glad to exit for the Olson hill as we got in the little bus to head for the course. The culprit in the stall was still not feeling good (I'm sure you know who he is), but he knew he had no choice but to compete or lose his position at the starting line. For those of you who don't know what I'm talking about, when we got lined up to run at a meet, we would be lined up by our coaches based on our times. It was usually Bernie 1st, Joey 2nd, Jony 3rd, etc., and the rest of the school 10th. Willard was 11th. So, if you know the twins very well, you know that there is very little competition between the two; they are very loving brothers who would do anything to make sure the other one looked like he was the best at whatever event they were competing in . . . NOT!!!! Joey was determined to not lose his position to Jony, so even though he was not feeling well he was bound and determined to kick his brother's butt.

We all got ourselves stretched out and prepared for the very scenic run. At times during the run you would see a gopher or twenty and the grass was a lovely shade of brownish green, which will be important later on . . . it helped hide the evidence. We got ourselves up to the starting line, and the gun sounded. Off like a turd of hurtles we went. I guess maybe that was me, the rest of the crew was out like a shot, as it's important to get out earlier to get a lead and get away from the pack . . .

As I had stated, everyone was off and runny, I mean running . . . as I also stated, I was following up the pack as usual, just enjoying the view that I had described to you earlier. On this course, at times you could see the other runners. Now believe this or not, some of this part may be an embellishment, but I'm telling the story and I'm sticking to it. As you ran down the fence line on the east side of the course, you could see down this valley where we had to come up and over this hill, and then you looped back up and would run into some runner who you may be lapping. Mind you, I didn't lap any of them. Anyway, I could see Joey had a pretty good lead on Jony. Now remember, Joey was not feeling well, he was feeling, should we say crappy!?! So it looked as if Joey thought he might be able to stop at the bottom of the hill and relieve himself. But just as he was starting to pull his shorts down, over the hill comes Jony. Joey hurries up, pulls up his shorts and takes off, I think feeling he could get a lead again and try it somewhere else along the course.

So I believe I was heading up the first hill when, behind me, here comes Joey, and again feeling like he has time to stop and release some pent-up energy or gas. Needless to say, Jony was not far behind still, so I think it was at this point that he decided he could maybe make it up the big hill and finish out and then run for the nearest open space. Well, that hill is a tough ol' climb, and you have to grunt to get up it. Well, if you haven't guessed by now, Joey had one too many grunts and soon left a trail that Hansel and Gretel could have followed. But in true competitive fashion, he did not allow Jony to beat him, and come Saturday morning, he was in the number-two spot, ready to take on the Frazer Bearcubs.

True story.

Two Questions

When I watched (in awe sometimes) Jon step up and play the way he did in the 1978 tournament run to State—step up like I had never seen him step up before—it was, to say the least, a little surprising to me as well. From the beginning, before District even started, Jon led the Panthers to State that year. He was the one that tacked up the "WIN" sign on our bedroom wall before the tournament started. He was the one that had the big game against Outlook semi-final night, scoring 22 points and raising his index finger high in the air in triumph late in the game after hitting the jump shot that put the nail in the coffin. It was Jon that had the big game against Richey semi-final night at Divisional, scoring 27 points and dominating the game. He stepped up big time in the challenge game against Flaxville in the fourth quarter too. Then, at State, well, he was voted MVP. Nothing more need be said on that count.

So, all of this begs two questions: What got into Jon in that 1978 tournament run? And why was I so much more competitive than Jon?

To answer the first question, we have to go back to semi-final night at District a year earlier, in 1977. This was when Westby beat

Jon Puckett, State Class C MVP, 1978
Helena Independent Record photo
by Bill Bowman.

us 72–70 in double-overtime. We lost to Antelope the next morning and were eliminated from the tournament. In the Westby game, I scored 42 points, and Jon had two. Two. Later that spring and summer, after the pain had worn off from the loss, I started to tease him about the game. "You know, Jon, if you would have scored three points in regulation, we would have went to Divisional. One lousy free throw from you and we go, that's it." And, "Sometimes I wonder if you took Coach Shaffer seriously when he said, 'It doesn't matter whether you win or lose, as long as you look good.'" Stuff like that. These barbs would later morph into my new nickname for Jon: "Four." Jon's nickname became "Four." I added two points to the Westby game because it seemed like whenever Jon didn't play well he would score four points. So I called him "Four," in honor of his dominating, game-altering performance against Westby at District semifinal night in 1977.

I think I might have got in his head a little. Jon had something to prove in 1978; he had carried that game he'd had against Westby the year before with him for an entire year, and he wasn't about to let it happen again. His performance in the tournament in 1977 motivated him—like nothing else ever had—to perform better in the 1978 tournament. And did he ever! In some ways, I think it was good we didn't make it to Divisional in 1977. It made us hungrier in 1978.

To answer the second question, why was I more competitive? Simple: I was the oldest twin by seven minutes. Dad expected a lot more out of me, demanded it, groomed it, and required it, me being the "oldest" #1 twin and all. It was that simple. How else do two genetically identical clones turn out to be so different?

One More Time in '79

Changes

A lot of changes for Peerless High School and for the Peerless Panthers in 1979. Marvin Hash, the superintendent at PHS since 1971, left to take another job in Oregon. He was a great superintendent, and was integral to things turning around for Peerless basketball. He left some big shoes to fill. Mr. Robert Harney became the new superintendent. He was a great guy, and did a great job, but there was something missing without Marvin Hash walking the halls of Peerless High School.

We also had a new coach. Coach Shaffer abandoned us (yes, I will use that word) to take the head coaching job at Charlo. Reminds me of a biblical quote in the New Testament: "And the Coach abandoned his players and fled . . ." or something like that, my knowledge of scripture is not that good. Seriously, we always wished Coach Clark Shaffer the best.

Our new coach was "Diamond" Jim Niccum, another great coach in a long line of great coaches to come to Peerless. He had coached at Scobey in 1977–78, and Opheim the season before that, so he was very familiar with our team. I remember at the start of the year when he was introduced as the new head coach, he told the student body, "If you can't beat 'em join 'em." I thought that was kind of odd to say because we had never beat the Opheim team or the Scobey teams he coached. Oh well, sounded good. To say that he was a character would be a massive understatement; oh, my God

1979 Peerless Panthers.

1979 Panther Cheerleaders.

this man was nuts, a real practical joker. His practices, however, were not so hilarious—he would work us to the bone. Very structured and disciplined, with enormous emphasis on conditioning, jumping, running, defense, you name it. Let's just say we were in shape and ready to play. Brian Bechtold, sane only by comparison, remained as our assistant coach.

We had new uniforms as well, at least new home uniforms. They were modeled after Marquette University's uniforms; Marquette won the NCAA championship in 1977. Their players would always wear their jerseys out (not tucked in), so their coach, Al Maguire, finally designed a jersey for them that would stay outside the trunks and never needed to be tucked in. Our home uniforms in 1979 were untucked and had "Peerless" running across the bottom of the jersey, rather than above the number in the middle. The NCAA would eventually ban this uniform design in 1984. Not sure if high schools ever did the same.

And we had lost two starters, Roger Trang and Bill Fladager, to graduation, both of whom played forward, although neither one was six foot tall. They were also our co-captains and leaders, and we were definitely going to miss them. So who would replace them? Our sixth and seventh men from the year before, Bernie Wasser (now a junior) and Ray Chapman, a senior. They were going to have to step up because they had some pretty big shoes to fill. And step up they would! Joel Dighans was returning at center as a junior, and of course, Jon and I at guard, our senior year. Joel, Jon and I had all been voted to the all-tournament team at State the previous year, with Jon as MVP. Just as we did in 1978, we had a solid core of ten players, so our second five challenged us every day in practice. Rick Wasser, Mike Mattson, Matt Fouhy, Brian Halverson and John Machart formed the second five, and freshman Dwane Dighans, Mike Machart, Wally Hames and Jamey Snare would round out the twelve Panthers suiting up at various times during the year. Those freshman would later play at State for the 1982 Panthers. Kelly Trang also played with us for part of the year.

And last, but certainly not least, our goal for the 1979 season had changed from the 1978 season. Now, instead of just *playing* in the State tournament, our goal had become *winning* the State tournament. We had raised the bar, the expectation was higher, and this expectation we put on ourselves would adversely affect the way we played later on in the year, as well as change our entire mindset regarding wins and losses in the tournaments. Related to this higher expectation, we were now regarded as one of the favorites, and not the underdogs anymore. We had been discovered; people knew who we were. At first I liked that, but now that I look back on it over 30 years later, I would pick being the underdog rather than the favorite any day. Playing *without* any expectation is much better than the alternative.

Running and Playing

For me, basketball season really started with cross country. I sort of looked at cross country as pre-season training for basketball, otherwise I probably never would have gotten through it. John Hebnes was our cross country coach, along with Brian Bechtold. We worked very hard every day after school. I hated it when we ran intervals around the baseball diamond! It was the Peerless version of the 440-yard dash, but I think it was little further. We would run cross country after school, then go home, eat dinner and come back up to the gym to play basketball every night. These games at night in the gym were the greatest time you could have playing basketball, just running up and down the court, fast breaking, shooting, having fun. These games could get competitive, but it wasn't as intense, not *nearly* as intense as when the season started. In some cases, we'd be trying to keep score, but then sometimes we would lose the score, forget about it. We'd just run up and down the court, playing basketball and having fun, and we would not even think about the score anymore. It was almost as if it were an endless game. I have the greatest memories of playing those games at night in the fall up at the Peerless Gym with my brother Jon and all my friends. Pure joy.

Well, the hard work in cross country paid off. Bernie Wasser won the individual State cross country championship that year and our team took third! Couldn't believe it when I crossed the finish line at the State cross country meet and someone came up to me and told me Bernie had won it! I knew he was a good runner, but I didn't think he was going to win it! Great experience for all of us. There were some people up at the gym when we got back to welcome us

Running cross country on the prairie of northeastern Montana, fall 1978. Pre-season training for the upcoming 1978-79 basketball season.

home (not quite as many as were there for basketball!), and Bernie gave a little speech. It was a great lead-in to the basketball season. State cross country was always the last part of October, and basketball practice started the first week in November. Nice to bring some more hardware back to Peerless right before the 1979 season began!

Basketball practice would start the following week. We thought we were in shape, you know, after running cross country and then playing basketball every night. So let's just go out now and play basketball, right? But Coach Niccum had other ideas . . .

A "Diamond" is Forever

Coach "Diamond" Jim Niccum. Unforgettable. Prior to 1978–79, Coach Niccum had coached at Opheim my sophomore year and then at Scobey my junior year. He knew our team up and down because we were 0–6 against him while he coached those two teams. And those two teams were good, I mean, *very* good teams. His Opheim team in 1976–77 (my sophomore season) was a power-house in 3-C. I don't think they lost a game in conference, they were rated in the State power polls, and everyone expected them to go to State and do well, maybe even win it. One of the best Opheim teams I ever saw, and they had some really good teams. They started Mark Stevens and Eric Tokerud at guard, John Jensen and Jeff Larson at forward, and Blake Anderson at center. Great team, great shooters, they had an inside-outside game, played great defense; and were well-coached by Niccum.

But they had a total meltdown, I mean a complete death spiral implosion at their District tourney that year in Glasgow. I can't remember who they lost to in the semi-final game, but it was an upset. No one had come close to them in conference that year. Then, in the morning game (Saturday morning upset!), they played Hinsdale. I don't think Hinsdale had come within 20 points of them during the season. I was listening to that game on the radio on Saturday morning because our tournament was the previous weekend (we had lost to Westby and then Antelope so we were done). I will never forget the end of that Opheim-Hinsdale game.

Coach "Diamond" Jim Niccum.
Helena Independent Record photo.

Opheim had an eight-point lead with 52 seconds left in the game . . . and lost the game! This was when there were no three-pointers either. It was unbelievable. They literally did everything they had to do to lose that game. It was as if they had scripted it. They missed free throws, turned the ball over, had defensive lapses, you name it. Hinsdale had whittled the lead down to two points with only a few seconds left in regulation, and Blake Anderson (a great center, and a super-nice guy) was shooting two free throws for Opheim. Forget making one of the free throws, all he had to do was hit the rim and the game was over. If he hit the rim, it would take a desperation heave from full court at the buzzer to tie the game because Hinsdale was out of timeouts. So what happened? He shot an air ball on the second free throw! Hinsdale got the ball out of bounds on the side, threw it in to someone up the court, and then turned and made a basket at the buzzer to send the game into overtime. Opheim was so shell-shocked that Hinsdale came out and scored the first four or six points in overtime and it was over. One of the best Opheim teams I ever saw never even made it out of their District. And Niccum was their coach . . .

My junior year, Coach Niccum moved from Opheim to coach at Scobey. Scobey had an incredibly good team that year; it was basically the same team that would win the State B championship the following year (1979), except they were all juniors. Danny Danelson, Gerry Veis, Don Boos, Brad Henderson, Martin Lantz (a senior), Kelly Norman, Scott Fjeld, Kirby Halvorson: they were all great players. We lost to them three times my junior year. Scobey ended up playing a challenge game to go to State B against Circle that year. They had beaten Circle badly both times that year, and were leading them in the challenge game, but Circle came back to beat them in the second half. I remember listening to that game on the radio, too, and I couldn't believe they lost. This was a Scobey team that had beaten Plentywood that year, and Plentywood would go onto win the State B championship with MVP Craig Guenther. Had Scobey made it to State that year, they very well could have won it. But they would have to wait another year, my senior year, to do that. That Circle game was another bitterly disappointing loss to end a season for Coach Niccum, just like the Opheim season. Everyone expected both of those teams to go to State and do well, but neither team even made it out of their District. High expectations with disappointing results, and tough, season-ending losses in the tournaments in both cases.

So why am I writing so much about Coach Niccum's previous two seasons? It helps to understand the pressure that was on him when he came to Peerless in 1978–79, when he inherited yet another team for which everyone had high expectations. We were expected to go to State and perhaps win it all. Do you think he could come into practice and be soft on us after what we had done the year before, and after what had happened to his teams the previous two seasons at Opheim and Scobey? After finishing third at State the previous year in 1978, we were returning three starters, three All-State players (Joe, Jon and Joel); and our other two starters, Bernie Wasser and Ray Chapman, had both seen action on the court in the consolation game against Wibaux at State as well. High expectations and two previous disappointing seasons for Niccum added up to some pretty intense practices for the Panthers beginning that first week in November, and carrying on throughout the entire season.

The Practical Joker and Comedian

Before I get into the 1979 season, just a few examples on what a character Coach Niccum was. He loved to play practical jokes. One day in class he had this cage up on his desk; you couldn't really see into it. He said it was his pet Mongoose. So he coaxed you up to have a look at this pet Mongoose because he was so proud of it, you know. But the only way you could see it was to peer closely up to the cage because the Mongoose was in the back of the cage where you could barely see it. He said, "Be careful because the Mongoose has a temper and is a little 'jumpy.' Don't startle it." He got you to peer in the cage, and then WHAM! he pressed some kind of button and this furry thing popped out of the cage right in your face with a big shriek! He got a few students on that one, myself included. Really got the heart pumping!

He played another practical joke on me later in the school year, after the tournaments were over. I was getting some calls from college coaches for recruiting and he knew that, so one morning he knocks on the door of Pat Haas' science class, interrupts the class and says "Joe, you have a telephone call in the teacher's lounge. I think it's the coach of a college." So I'm feeling pretty important, you know, getting to walk out of class and take this phone call from a recruiter. I walk into the teacher's lounge. There is a phone on the desk with the receiver off the hook. I sit down, pick up the phone and say "Hello." Nothing on the other end. Not a peep. Then I look down at the phone and it's not even plugged into the wall! I look back at the door to the lounge and there stands Niccum with his head peeking around the corner and this big impish smile on his face, his eyes sparkling like a kid who got exactly what they wanted for Christmas!

Niccum also scripted his own hilarious skits for pep rallies. One of the things he would do would be to play Carnac the Magnificent, a character Johnny Carson played on the Tonight Show. On the Tonight Show, Carson (Carnac) would hold an envelope up to his head, and then predict the answer to the question in the envelope. Brian Bechtold would play Ed McMahon. McMahon would always repeat the Carnac's answer. So Niccum holds this envelope up to his head at one pep rally and says, "Bernie Wasser, Joe Puckett and Scag Anderson." Bechtold repeats it, then Niccum opens the envelope and reads the question: "Name a runner a gunner and a funner." That's just one of them!

Boot Camp

A typical Jim Niccum practice for the 1978–79 Panthers was very structured, intense, with a heavy emphasis on defense and physical conditioning. Most coaches would run you pretty good that first month in November, but Niccum continued that all the way through the season. He even ran us on the practices on the way down to State tournament in Helena at Northern Montana College! I remember there were some Army Reservists in the NMC gym while we were practicing; they looked at us running with their eyes wide open and thought, "Man, I'm glad I'm in the Army and not playing for *that* coach!"

We'd start each practice with 100 tip-toe jumps, with our arms high in the air. Niccum would be out in front of us and he'd jumping on his toes too. Then we'd break into defensive shuffle, left, right, back, forward, and he'd be out in front again, pointing the direction he wanted us to go. Next, we'd break out and do power jumps for a minute, two sets. These are really hard if you've never done them. What he'd have us do is get underneath one of the baskets, right underneath the net, and then jump as high as we could, driving up with both arms and touching the net on both sides as high as we could. We'd have a partner, and tradeoff the sets. We would do this twice. Then we'd run a couple line drills; they always came in twos. We'd probably run 12–14 of these in any given practice, more in some cases, depending on how lousy we played. We would also do a defensive denial drill, which really made you shuffle your feet. He'd stand on one side of the court and Bechtold would be on the other, and we'd have to deny the entry pass on the wing for the person we were guarding. The offensive player would run across the court, back and forth, and we'd have to deny the ball on the wing so the pass could not get through. At the end, we'd have to let the pass get through and then play one on one.

We also did a lot of rebounding block-out drills, with the ball in the middle and keeping our man out and away from the ball. The drills I just mentioned—running, jumping, defense, rebounding—we would do these *every* practice. Niccum would also have us run our offense to perfection in the half court set. But once every practice, somewhere in the middle, we got to run our favorite drill. This was 3 on 2 fast break drill, called the Blitz Drill. There would be two defenders on each end of the court, and three offensive players would attack 3 on 2, and then, when a shot was made, or there was a steal or a rebound, the play would go the other way, with 3 attackers against 2. This would run continuously. It was our favorite drill because we just got to run up and down and fast break like we did at night in the fall, playing pickup games. When we did this drill, Coach Niccum would sit on the top row of the bleachers in the middle of the gym and coach us from up there. Never wanted that drill to end, it was so much fun! But if I remember right, we'd break into a couple more line drills when it was done, so maybe that was why!

Coach Niccum's coaching style was like that of Tommy Lasorda, former manager of the Los Angeles Dodgers. Niccum would *really* cheer us on, clap his hands together furiously and yell really loud encouraging things to us. I really liked that about him. He could also get in your grill—just ask a few players on the team about that! But I liked playing for him, and I think he worked us as hard as he did because he knew what the high expectations for our team were. He was not about to let this team disappoint like his two previous teams at Opheim and Scobey had done.

The Top Ten that Wasn't

Midway through November, as our grueling practices with Niccum continued, I started to look ahead and get really excited about our first game in the Nashua Tournament against Opheim. But my excitement for that first game could not *nearly* match the excitement I had upon seeing the pre-season State Class C Power Poll rankings.

My entire life growing up in Peerless, I had looked at those rankings, and had never seen Peerless crack the top ten. I think a couple times—as Peerless would tend to upset eventual State champions in conference and in District now and again—we would be one of those "others receiving votes" teams, you know. But that didn't count. There were no numbers 1–10 in front of Peerless in the rankings. Also, I was tired of being the underdog, and after taking third at State in 1978, and with three All-State starters returning, I was looking forward to a little respect for Peerless when I read the rankings.

There had to be two possibilities: 1) Peerless was going to be ranked number one in the Pre-Season Power Poll. We were the logical choice. Who were you going to rank ahead of us? Outlook had lost Selvig, Wangerin and West to graduation. I had checked the 1978 State tournament program, and all the teams there had lost their best players to graduation, including Manhattan Christian. Or 2) If we were not going to be ranked number one, who was? The only team I could think of was Flaxville, because they were returning Kevin Hatfield as a senior, who had been voted MVP in State as a freshman in 1976 when Flaxville won it; and the state remembered him. Flaxville had been ranked high in 1977, only losing one game the entire season up to Divisionals, where they lost the championship to Antelope and then lost a challenge game to Richey. Plus, we had beaten Flaxville in a challenge game the previous year, 1978, to make it to State, so everyone knew they had a good team.

Who would it be? I looked and looked and looked and watched the Billings Gazette in November and . . . no rankings came. Then, to my incredible disbelief, Dad told me that in the year 1979, there would be *no State Power Poll* rankings What? Are you kidding me? Why? The answer was the MHSA decided that teams were running up scores in regular season games to get higher rankings, so if they didn't post the rankings coaches would start substituting more and stop running up the scores. Well, so much for rankings.

Hubris and Humility

When I wrote about the 1978 Panthers, I pretty much started right before District tournament, but I'm going to pick up a little earlier with the 1979 Panthers, as in the very first game of the season. Normally I wouldn't write about a game this early in the season: What could it have to do with the rest of the season, right? Answer: Everything. Our first game against Opheim in Nashua's Invitational Tournament would fundamentally and radically alter the way our team played for the rest of the season (for the good). It was, absolutely, the best way the season could have started, although it didn't seem that way at the time. So it definitely needs to be discussed.

It was quite a feeling running out onto the court for our first game in Nashua. The last time we had taken the court was against Wibaux in the consolation game at State in March, and I remembered it well. Plus, this was the beginning of my senior year, so this was it. This was the last "first game" I would ever have as a Peerless Panther. I was pretty pumped, both emotionally and physically. Our new coach, "Diamond" Jim Niccum, had us in unbelievable shape. Even after the grueling cross country season, our team's physical conditioning had been taken to another level by his demanding practices.

I remember the announcer at Nashua actually introduced us as the third place team from State in 1978. He really got into it, and I thought that was pretty cool. The previous year, no one knew who we were, and now everyone did; I liked that. I didn't realize at the time, however, that it is much more fun to play as the underdog, with no expectation placed upon you, than it is to play as the favorite. Now, after looking back on it, I would pick being the underdog any day. I think the rest of the 1979 Peerless Panthers would agree with me.

So how did these highly touted, high-powered Panthers do in their very first game against Opheim? Well, for the first three quarters, miserably. Opheim started a very tall lineup, 6'6" Norm Dyrland, 6'3" Rick Maus, 6'4" Brent Lawrence, 6'1" Kevin St. John and then Randy Stolen at guard. We didn't have anyone six-foot tall, of course, so to compensate for that—just as Coach Shaffer had done the year before—Niccum had us come out in a 2-1-2 zone, and we stayed in it for three quarters. And after three quarters, we were trailing Opheim 32–31.

So much for an aura of invincibility.

I started to get frustrated with the Opheim players. I felt like they weren't showing us any respect. I was thinking, "Hey, don't you know who we *are*? Don't you know what we've accomplished?" And then, after three quarters, I realized, this was a new season, and teams weren't going to roll over and die for us just because we were the Peerless Panthers. The humble feeling I had running out onto the court for the fourth quarter was a little different than the powerful feeling I had felt when I ran out to start the game: Now, after all the hype, we were in a fight to just to win our first game of the season in 1979.

For three quarters in that zone, we would trot back on defense. Opheim's guards would sloooowly bring the ball up the court, and we would make sure to keep one foot in the paint to protect the middle. Opheim didn't have much for outside shooters, so we just stayed back in that zone. Their guards would dribble to one side and pass, then bring it back to the other and pass, back and forth, over and over. And in the meantime, this superbly conditioned, lightening-quick Panther team, a team that had run across the frozen tundra of Northeast Montana all fall (nimbly dodging cow pies and gopher holes along the way), basically stayed back in that zone and let Opheim dictate the tempo of the game. Opheim extended their lead in the fourth quarter, and so Niccum brought us out of that zone to put pressure on the ball. This is where the game turned, just like so many of the games the previous year had turned, when we would come out and pressure the ball and press. We started pressing and getting some turnovers, and then started fast breaking off the turnovers like we knew how to do. We broke loose for 24 points in the fourth quarter—almost matching our total from the previous three—and won the game going away 55-45, outscoring Opheim 24–13 in the final quarter. You have no idea the contrast between the fourth quarter and the first three quarters. It was like getting let out of a cage, and I duly noted that feeling, a feeling that was going to be communicated to my dad later that night.

So, our first game against Opheim taught us three things:

1) We needed to fight for wins just like we always had in previous seasons; it wasn't going to be easy.

2) We needed to get out of our zone defense and play man-to-man to exploit our strength, rather than to protect our weakness.

3) Opheim had a really good team and were extremely well coached with Loren Baker. We would see this team again, semi-final night at Divisionals, where we would come within a few harrowing seconds of not advancing to State our senior year . . .

Proposal and Acceptance

That night at home, Dad and I had a little talk. I told him my frustration over staying back in zones and letting the other team dictate the tempo of the game. Our greatest strength, I believed, was our superior speed and quickness. When we played zones, that strength was cut off at the knees. "Why not," I asked Dad, "dictate the tempo of the game with our *defense*?" Let's not wait until we get the ball to attack with our fast break, let's attack right out of the gate with an intense, man-to-man defense, take it right at them, and use our superior conditioning and quickness to our advantage, before we even get the ball. Why wait?" The other side of the argument was, "Yeah, that's great, but what happens when three guys 6'5" get the ball on the block matched up against Joel, Bernie and Ray underneath? What then?" My answer to that was: "I'll take my chances with Dighans down there any day. He can take care of himself. And besides, that's our last line of defense anyway. First, we don't let them get the ball past half court with our full court man-to-man pressure. If they break that, we pressure the ball in the half court and then deny the ball to the wings so they can't enter their offense. Then, if they get the ball inside, we collapse and help each other out.

And occasionally, Dighans swats one back out of there to start our fast break going the other way."

I convinced Dad. (Don't you think it was a convincing argument?) Perhaps the servant had become the master? No, never. But the next step was to convince Niccum it was the right thing to do. That was not going to be easy. Niccum liked to play zones. We had played his Opheim and Scobey teams six times the previous two years, and I remember seeing some form of zone defense against his teams every game, usually a 2–1-2 or 2–3. We were 0–6 against his Opheim and Scobey teams those two years. Okay Dad, don't bring *that* up! So Dad had a beer or two with Niccum that night at the local pub in Peerless and proposed the defensive alteration, and it was decided that the next night against Nashua the 1979 Panthers would come out in a full court, man-to-man defense, and stick with it the entire game.

The next night, the cage was opened and we came out man-to-man all the way up and down the court. If our man went to the bathroom, we followed him in there. Okay, not really, but the result? Nashua (a very good team by the way) scored only 23 points in the first three quarters, and we blew them out 80–55, pestering and harassing their guards incessantly all over the court, forcing numerous turnovers and playing pressure defense the whole game. It was pure Joy. Run and run and run, the way basketball was meant to be played.

The First Beer Séance

Sunday night, the fundamental shift in defensive strategy for the 1979 Panthers was officially sealed in what I'll label a late-night beer séance at the Puckett house, with Tiny Puckett and "Diamond" Jim Niccum. The 1979 Peerless Panthers would not play another possession of zone defense the rest of the season—would not practice it, would not talk about it, would not even think about it. Would it catch up with us against Flaxville at Divisional and State championship? Maybe so, but we were going to attack with our strength rather than protect our weakness, and that is how the 1979

Panthers played: If you were going to beat us, you were going to beat us at our game, not yours, and that gave us the initiative.

So in 1979, we said goodnight, and sweet dreams forever to the zone defense. And it was a blessing that we had played a good Opheim team our first game of the season. It was definitely a wakeup call. The 1979 Panthers were now awake.

Playing Up

Of all the things that could be written or said about the 1979 Panthers, playing a soft non-conference schedule could not be one of them. After the Nashua tournament (Opheim and Nashua would finish 1–2 in District 3-C that year), our third game was against Class B Plentywood at Plentywood. Plentywood had won the Class B State championship the previous year, with Craig Guenther, who had transferred from Antelope, the MVP. Guenther was the same age as Jon and me; he was a senior that year, just as we were, and Plentywood was returning many other players who had played the year before as well. We played on a Thursday night in Plentywood, so there were a lot of kids from Sheridan County there, from Westby, Antelope and Medicine Lake. They got an eyeful that night, as we beat Plentywood on their home court, 54–44, breaking the game open in the last three minutes with our man-to-man pressure, and running our record to 3–0. This was a very good Plentywood team, and we handled them pretty well. They would end up taking second at State that year in Class B, losing to Scobey. It was strange playing Guenther in a Plentywood uniform, as I had played against him since fifth grade, when he was playing for Dagmar and then Antelope. Plentywood was coached by Zoonie McLean, a coaching legend, and it was an honor to be playing on the same court where he was coaching. That set up the first of three classic matchups with the Class B Scobey Spartans the next night at Scobey. The Spartans were a powerful team that would go onto to win their first Class B championship later that year.

A Spartan Challenge

Playing at Scobey that next night was exciting. The fans in Daniels County knew these two teams were superb, and they were looking forward to a spectacular game. And the teams did not disappoint. We played very well as a team that night; we ended up with four players in double figures. I got in foul trouble in the first half and had to sit out, and then again at the end of the third quarter when I got my fourth foul. In the first half, I got a technical foul called on me after Danny Danelson fell back on a charge. I didn't think that I had touched him that hard; nevertheless, the ref called a foul on me, my third foul. Because I knew it was my third foul and I'd have to sit out, I lost my temper on the court. I didn't think I'd fouled him. The Scobey fans erupted after I got that T.

We led for most of the game, including at halftime and at the end of the third quarter, right up until the last minute when Danelson hit a free throw to put them ahead, and then a field goal after that to put them up by three. Final score was 66–63, our first loss of the season. Scobey's team that year was amazingly good, with Danny Danelson, Gerry Veis, Don Boos, Brad Henderson, Kelly Norman, Kirby Halvorson and Scott Fjeld. They were the best team I ever played in my high school career. They were also very well coached by Tom Hagadon. In 1979, they would only lose to Class A Sidney, 55–54. I remember listening to that game on the radio in our locker room in Peerless before a game we were going to play. I thought to myself, as I heard the end of that game on the radio, "That's probably the only game Scobey is going to lose this year," and I was right. They stormed through their conference and pummeled everyone they played at State, including Plentywood in the championship. Great team, great guys, and of course, Kelly Norman was our informant, constantly gathering intelligence for us on our rival Flaxville constantly. A huge asset for the Panthers, was Kelly Norman.

The next weekend we played Scobey again, this time at home in Peerless. The Peerless gym was packed to overflowing capacity as the Daniels County fans came out once again to watch another showdown between these top teams in the state. And once again they got their money's worth. This time, unlike at Scobey the week before, Scobey led the entire game, from the opening tip until the final seconds of regulation. They had a six point lead at the end of the third quarter, but then we came back in the fourth quarter, trailing by two points, and we had possession of the ball with just a few seconds left. The seconds were winding down. We took one shot on the basket, then another, and kept getting the offensive rebound, and then finally, right at the buzzer, Bernie Wasser got a rebound on the right side and swished about a ten-foot jumper to tie it just as the buzzer sounded! We were going into overtime with Scobey! In the overtime, Scobey made a single free throw to take the lead by one, and then we were coming down the court with a chance to take the lead with just about a minute left. I had a decent look at the basket but couldn't get the shot to fall. Scobey got the rebound and we had to foul. They made their free throws, and the game ended 63–59 for Scobey.

Sometimes I look back on those games against Scobey and wonder how we ever even played with those guys, after what they did to Class B teams the rest of the season; just decimated them. I remember talking to a player from Three Forks in my dorm room at Carroll College the next year, my freshman year, and we were talking about basketball and Scobey's team. He played for Three Forks the previous year, when Scobey had absolutely destroyed them in the semi-final at the State B tourney. I'm pretty sure Three Forks was undefeated at the time and Scobey just rocked them. Anyway, I told him we had played Scobey tough in two games, with a chance to beat them both times, and he said to me, incredulously, "*How did you do that?*" He couldn't believe another team could even play with them. Then I told him we beat Plentywood and he couldn't believe that either! It is said that the only way the three Daniels County teams could have won the State championship that year was if Scobey had played in Class A and Peerless or Flaxville competed in Class B.

Bah Humbug!

Now, although our scheduler that year had done well scheduling Opheim for our first game of the season, that same scheduler should not have invited Scobey to our annual Peerless Christmas Invitational Tournament (PCIT, pronounced "PEESIT") at Christmastime. Everyone knows you invite teams to tournaments that you can beat, not the other way around! In fact, I never had a Merry Christmas my entire high school career. Well, okay, maybe that's a slight exaggeration, because sometimes Santa Claus would help take the sting out a loss right before Christmas, but he had to come through pretty big to do it. You know, like a brand new 8-track tape player or something like that, with a couple of kickass 8-tracks to go with it, like KISS Greatest Hits, and maybe a greatest hits collection by Queen as well. AC/DC would be right up there too. In 1977, when I was a sophomore, we played Opheim in our PCIT championship and they beat us soundly. They were a very good team who should have made it to State that year. Bah! Humbug! Then, the following year we played Scobey for the championship of the PCIT and they pounded us 82–69. Bah Humbug again! Then, my senior year, we again had to play Scobey for the championship of the PCIT. Double Bah Humbug!

Busgate

But before I write about the championship game of the PCIT against Scobey, we played the Bainville Bulldogs in the first game of the tourney. Now, it turns out that some of us on our team had a bit of a tainted past with Bainville, which was related to what later became known as the infamous "Busgate" scandal. Whenever this incident came up in the Puckett house, Dad would always say to me, "That wasn't your finest hour Joey." In hindsight, it may have been my darkest hour.

So what happened? Five years earlier, in early October, 1974, my eighth-grade year, the Peerless Pink Panthers, our girls basketball team, were playing the Bainville Bulldogs in a non-conference contest at Peerless. The game started out innocently enough, but as the game wore on, it became increasingly apparent that the Bainville team was very physical, and they were roughing our girls up pretty good. Bernie Wasser (a seventh-grader at the time) was sitting on the bottom row of the bleachers in the Peerless Pep Club section, and he started to heckle the Bainville girls a little bit. Then some of the rest of us started to chime in, and went downhill from there. The Bainville girls were looking over at our section and started to jaw back at us a little, even as they were playing on the court.

Well, at the end of the third quarter, Bernie had had enough, so he went home and raided his mom Phyllis' refrigerator and brought back a dozen eggs. When the game ended, and as the Bainville girls were leaving the court, the jawing continued on both ends. Wasser left the gym with the eggs, and somehow I ended up with a few of those eggs in my hand as well, and, along with Wasser, we proceeded to egg Bainville's bus while their girls were showering. Somebody blew the whistle on us, and we ended up scattering out to a stubble field just north of our high school, looking back at the scene of the crime as we ran. We were ducking down in the stubble looking and listening to what was being said in the crisp autumn air, even as the crime was discovered. Voices were becoming pretty loud and emotional. We started to hear things like "It was Bernie Wasser and Joe Puckett! We saw them do it! They're out there in that stubble field!" Oh no! What were we going to do? Run away and everything would be okay? So I came back to the front door of the school, where several Panther students were massed. There was quite a buzz going, you know, as this was quite a happening; it's not every night an opposing girls basketball team's bus gets egged in Peerless.

Well, this was not the type of thing you wanted to do under Marvin Hash's rule. I had really, really done it this time. Later the next week, a letter came from the superintendent of Bainville High School addressed to Marvin Hash, something about "In over 30 years of school administration, I have never seen anything so appalling . . ." you know, something like that. The letter got posted up in the hallway of the school for everyone to see. Thankfully, I

Peerless and Bainville leaving the court following their PCIT game, 1978.

didn't get suspended. As punishment, we had to write a letter to the Bainville girls basketball team apologizing for the incident. What I wrote was very sincere. Then, I had to attend a school board meeting and apologize to the school board, of which my dad was a member, and Marvin Hash for what I'd done.

The Forgiven

So Bernie and I thought we might be marked men running out onto that court against Bainville, even though the incident had occurred some five years earlier. We had written letters to their school apologizing for the bus incident, but we weren't sure if all was forgiven.

Well, it did turn out that this was a physical game, a very physical game, but Bainville was not playing with a grudge; it was just the way they normally played. They had a good football program, and most of those guys on that team were tough, very tough farm boys (you could just tell). They got in there and mixed it up pretty good.

Peerless in its man-to-man defense versus Scobey, PCIT championship, 1978.

We blew them out 75–33, but Bainville outplayed us in certain aspects of the game, like "Loose balls pounced on as if it were a fumble recovery" and "Sacks on the shooter." In the end, Wasser and I escaped from the game virtually unscathed, and all was forgiven with Busgate.

No Charm

The championship game against Scobey, was one of those games where they put chairs along the sides of the wall of the Peerless gym so more people could see the game. I honestly did not want to play this team a third time. I felt we didn't really have anything left to learn by playing them again, and those two previous matchups were so close, with spectacular finishes, that with a third contest it would be hard to meet that standard. And that was exactly the case. We led after the first quarter, but after that, Scobey dominated us the rest of the way. They had so many talented players on that team, and on that night, our informant Kelly Norman would take it to the Peerless Panthers, scoring 18 points. Don Boos would have 16. Danny

Danny Danelson shoots against Peerless, PCIT championship, 1978.

Danelson and Gerry Veis, Scobey's two leading scorers, would not score 20 points between them that night, and yet Scobey still stuck it to us, demonstrating the incredible depth that team had. Hats off to the 1979 Scobey Spartans, State Class B champions, the finest team I ever played during my high school career. And Bah Humbug to our scheduler!

Christmas Reflection

So when Santa Claus came on Christmas day in 1978, as he always did, I had a lot to be thankful for, even though I didn't get the new 8-Track tape player I wanted. Although we had lost to Scobey three times before Christmas, our record was 7–3, and we had beaten a very good Plentywood team along the way. Christmas was always a pivotal time of the season. We had finished half of the season, and then we started to look ahead to the conference games, like the matchups we would have against Flaxville after playing them in the challenge game to make it to State the previous year; and Outlook, what would they be like with Doug Selvig, but without Randy Wangerin, Jerry West and Dave Selvig?

I also started to think more seriously about our team goals, like winning the Conference championship, the District championship, Divisional championship and the State championship, all for the first time in Peerless basketball history. Yes, this was our goal: A perfect conference record and then a clean sweep through all the tournaments. We did not expect to lose another game the rest of the year, now that Scobey was behind us, and anything short of standing on the podium to receive the gold medal at State in Helena in March would be a complete disappointment. We were going for gold; it was as simple as that.

Here are the results of the first ten games of the season for the 1979 Peerless Panthers:

> Peerless 55 Opheim 45 W
> Peerless 80 Nashua 55 W
> Peerless 54 Plentywood 44 W
> Peerless 63 Scobey 66 L
> Brockton 42 Peerless 82 W
> Scobey 63 Peerless 59 (OT) L
> Peerless 81 Med Lake 39 W
> Antelope 34 Peerless 79 W
> Bainville 33 Peerless 75 W
> Scobey 58 Peerless 45 L

A noticeable trend in these games is that in the six games we had played against Class C teams before Christmas, we had beaten them by an average margin of victory of 34 points, and only Nashua had scored over 50 points on us, and that was after our starting five sat on the bench the entire fourth quarter. Our dominance over Class C teams would continue as the conference season began in earnest the first week in January, when we would start our push toward Helena, one more time in '79 . . .

Jon Puckett guards Russell Edwards, Peerless vs. Flaxville at Peerless, 1979.
In the foreground, Matt Fouhy is defending Mike Safty.

A Cardinal New Year

And so, as we began "The Big Push" toward Helena (as Dad would call it), against whom do you suppose our first game of the New Year would be? None other than our archrival Flaxville, of course, and at home in Peerless. The last time we had faced Flaxville was in the challenge game in Wolf Point the year before, where we upset them to earn Peerless' first ever trip to State. But this was a different year; we had broken their seven-game win streak against us, and now it was our turn to be Kings of the Hill. Scobey had beaten Flaxville badly both times they had played them earlier that year, both at Flaxville and at Scobey; however, Flaxville didn't lose to them a third time because their schedulers knew better than to schedule Scobey for a Christmas tournament.

We were very pumped to take on Flaxville again. We knew they would have a great team. Flaxville's Kevin Hatfield was now a senior, and he had some good players around him, like David

Weltikol, Russell Edwards, Jesse Cook and Mike Safty. The big question mark for Flaxville that year was going to be their guard play. Who was going to replace those two very fine guards, Wade and Cory Tryan, who had been their steady backcourt the previous two years? The answer to that question was Rocky Nelson, who had not played much previously but would now have to step up and be their point guard. He improved steadily as the year went on, and turned into a very fine point guard by the end of the year. Most importantly for Flaxville, he learned how to handle our pressure, and thus minimized our greatest strength against this team.

In that first game against Flaxville at Peerless—the first of five games we would play against them that year—they came out and took the lead at the end of the first quarter, 14–9, shutting our high-powered offense down in the process. One of the things I realize now about Flaxville, as I look back on all of the games we played against them, is that they were an excellent defensive team. Coach Terry Bakken had his team play a very sticky, collapsing, helping, man-to-man defense, and we always had trouble attacking it. But in the second quarter, just like we had done in the fourth quarter against them the previous year at the challenge game, our pressure defense and fast break broke open the game, and we scored 25 points in the second quarter, outscoring them 25–8 in the process, and taking a 12-point lead at halftime. We controlled the game the second half; they started fouling us, and I made 17 of 19 free throws to seal it. We ended up winning 65–58, retaining our King of the Hill status over them, for the time being at least . . .

A New Outlook

The next noteworthy conference game that year was against Outlook, with Doug Selvig, now a junior, leading the defending State Champion Outlook Blue Jays. His supporting cast was good, with Kevin Ordahl at guard and Les Sebastian at center; but they were not nearly the team they were the year before with Wangerin, West and older brother Dave, although Doug's team would win the State championship the following year in 1980 against Opheim, the same

Opheim team (now juniors) that would give us fits at Divisionals. We handled Outlook quite easily at Peerless, winning 60–42. We were steamrolling at that point toward an undefeated conference season, but Flaxville and Outlook would only lose to each other in conference play, so we would have to beat Flaxville and Outlook on the road the final week of the conference season in order to clinch Peerless' first ever Conference championship . . .

Pronghorn Memories

But before I get into the final week of conference play against Flaxville and Outlook, I have to write a little bit about how sad it was playing Antelope that year. Prior to the 1978–79 season, the Antelope school and gym burned down, so they were playing their home games on Plentywood's home court. It was the strangest thing, playing Antelope in the Plentywood gym in a conference game. The gym was not that full, you know, it was just Peerless vs. Antelope in a conference game. Of course, Antelope's fans were there in force, as were their cheerleaders and pep club, wearing all the purple and gold colors, but it just didn't seem the same. And then, Craig Guenther, their leader and best player, the heart and soul of their Eastern Divisional winning 1977 team, had transferred to Plentywood the year before, so their team was not that strong. This was really the beginning of the end for 1-C as it once was. The Antelope school would close soon after this.

Fine basketball tradition, Antelope had. They were always competitive in the conference, and took second in State to Westby in 1975, losing only to Alan Nielsen and Westby that year. Their gym was quonset-shaped, and I loved playing there. It might have been smaller than the Peerless old gym; because the court was so narrow on the wings you were automatically in shooting range when you got the ball. We had a lot of shootouts with Guenther in that gym. I remember a junior high game where the score ended up 55–54, pretty high scoring for 7th and 8th graders.

One of the memories I had of playing Antelope in their gym epitomizes the spirit of small Class C teams in northeastern Montana. After the starting five for the varsity team were announced, all five starters, along with some substitutes and a couple cheerleaders, ran up onto stage behind the basket, grabbed their instruments, and then proceeded to play a rousing rendition of the National Anthem with the rest of the band. Then, after the song was over, the cheerleaders and basketball players jumped back down onto the court from the stage to cheer and to play the game. The Antelope fans were all so proud of their school, pulling together as they did to have both a band and a basketball team, and very fine cheerleaders as well. So here's to the Antelope Pronghorns, I will never forget your gym or your fine basketball tradition. Thanks for the memories . . .

Two Birds with One Stone

Going into that final week of conference at the end of January, we were 8–0 in conference, and both Flaxville and Outlook were 6–2. Outlook and Flaxville had split their conference games. We had beaten each of them at home, so if we lost both games, the conference would have ended in a three-way tie. But this isn't what we had in mind. All we had to do was win one game in order to clinch the first Conference championship in our school's 46-year history, but we planned to win them both and go undefeated. We played Flaxville first, and as we walked into their gym, we could feel the intensity of the heated rivalry in the air. There was a big "BEAT PEERLESS" sign draped opposite the side of the gym where we were sitting, and I thought that was a little audacious. This would be a tough game, but we led at every quarter break and made a strong run at the end of the third quarter—again brought on by our pressure defense—to take a 40–29 lead going into the fourth quarter.

It was an incredible feeling running out onto the court to start the fourth quarter. We were just eight minutes away from our school's first Conference championship in 46 years, and the Peerless fans were aware of that too, not just us players. The gym was rocking on both sides with the traditional "Go Cards Go!" and "Go

Panthers Go!" We finished the game strong, making seven of eight free throws in the end and winning 57–47. Bernie Wasser had his best game of the season for us that night; always coming through in the clutch, was Bernie, just like he had done in the challenge game the year before. He scored 17 points and led a balanced attack of four Panthers in double figures to lead Peerless to its first ever conference championship.

It is funny the things you remember. The next night we played Outlook at Outlook, our last conference game. I remember the bus ride to Outlook. We were all so relaxed, laughing and having a good time, having just clinched the conference championship. We wanted to go undefeated and take it to Outlook that night, but first we were going to enjoy the feeling of being champs for the first time. The thing I remember most about that bus ride was that Armand Fladager had a boom box of some sort, and he was playing Toto's first album, self-titled *Toto*. The song he played that night on the bus as we approached Outlook was, "Hold the Line." I will always associate that song with Peerless winning that conference championship in 1979, and beating Outlook to go undefeated in conference.

The first thing I did when I walked into Outlook's hallowed gym that night was look into their trophy case to see their State championship trophy from the previous year. There it was, centered right in the middle of the trophy case, with the nets draped around it. The ultimate symbol of success for the town that had the finest basketball tradition in District 1-C. And I thought, as I stood there admiring it, that this year that trophy was going to be ours.

Outlook was sky-high up for us that night, just as every team that year was, now that we were the team to beat. They came out, as they always did, and started running circles around us in that crazy gym of theirs. Doug Selvig (nicknamed "Rinky" by his teammates) and the boys took an 8–0 lead on us before Niccum finally called a timeout to settle us down. We came back out from the timeout and started to work our offense. We were trailing by only one point at the end of the first quarter. Amazingly, Jon held Doug Selvig to a single point in the first half. We led by three at half and by five at the end of the third quarter, and then we opened it up in the fourth quarter, with our fans bringing us on home to an undefeated conference season, outscoring Outlook 20–13 and winning the game going away 57–45. So, a perfect 10–0 in conference and Conference Champs! Our first goal had been met! Now, the only thing between us and the District tournament, the official beginning of the March to Helena, was two non-conference games the following weekend against Lambert and Froid.

We'll to the Gym No More

The Lambert game at Peerless was the last home game for Jon, Ray Chapman, Ricky Wasser, Mike Mattson and me; and it would also be a very emotional night for Dad, Jon and me. I can remember the four times I was most emotional as a Peerless Panther, and this is the first one, my last home game. The second (and most) emotional I've ever been was after losing to Flaxville in the State championship game. The third time was when it was announced that Jon and I were having our jerseys retired at the Athletic Banquet in the spring of 1979. The fourth time was at the State tournament in 1995, during the pep rally just before the State championship game when Peerless played Belt; and Jon and I gave a speech, along with the 1982 and 1988 Panther teams that had also been to State. Dad was there, and it was like a big Peerless Panther basketball reunion.

I had the strangest routine before home basketball games. It would always be the same. The Muppets Show would usually play in the late afternoon on TV before I would go up to the gym. So I would always watch this show because it relaxed me, and because I thought it was hilarious, with Kermit the Frog, Miss Piggy and the gang. Actually my favorite characters were the Swedish Chef and Beaker. Armand Fladager liked Beaker too; I remember he did a great Beaker impersonation. Dad would watch it with me if he was there, and I think he kind of got a kick out of watching my strange routine as well. Dad had got Jon and me fired up for the Lambert game (as he would always do) because he said he had heard through the grapevine that the folks in Lambert were calling Nick Vaira, a sophomore, the best guard in the State, because he was averaging

139

about 25 points a game or something like that. It was going to be me who was going to guard him, and there was a lot of pride on the line, because of course Dad thought Jon and I were the best guards in the State that year.

My heart was heavy the night we played Lambert at home. Part of the reason I was so sad was because I knew it was the end of an era for Dad, Jon and me. Our lives and relationships with each other were so intertwined with basketball that it was impossible at that point to imagine our lives without it. And this game would be the last time we would go up to that venerable gym and play a game on our home court, the last time we would come back home after the game to talk about it.

As was tradition on Senior Night, each senior would present his mother a bouquet of flowers when introduced before the game. It was especially poignant for me when Jon and I presented Mom her flowers at this ceremony. Mom had been the steady supporter of the dream through all those years, beginning in third grade when Dad first began coaching us. She had to be the patient one, standing aside and letting the boys "have their fun." I remember so many times when we would play basketball in the fall at the gym at night, after cross country practice. She would make sure she had dinner on the table immediately after practice so we had time enough to digest our food before we went back up to the gym and played basketball for two hours. That is just one example of a thousand. You never saw any "Soccer Mom" bumper stickers on cars in northeastern Montana. If we'd had any bumper sticker on our car, it would have read "Basketball Mom."

The game itself was a blowout; we were ahead 39–14 at halftime and won 76–41. I did a good job defensively against Vaira. He was scoreless at halftime, I think, and he got a lot of points late in the game when it was garbage time. I remember talking to him at half court on a free throw in the second half. He said something about the bus ride up to Peerless being so long and that they were tired, and I was like "Yeah, right," or something like that. Amazing how competitive I was back then. Nick Vaira was an extremely good player, and probably did very well his junior and senior year.

After the game, I showered and came home. It was very emotional in the Puckett house. I remember walking through the door and collapsing in Dad's arms, crying like a child, knowing that this was the last time we would have this experience together. Part of the reason I was so sad was for Dad; I knew that Jon and I might have a chance to play basketball in college, and that he could come and watch us play there (which he did), but it wouldn't be the same. And it wasn't. There was nothing like the experience of walking up to the Peerless Gym, playing a basketball game, and then walking home to talk about it with Dad and Jon, stopping at the Puckett Mercantile (my dad's store) along the way to grab a pepperoni pizza. It doesn't get any better than that!

Finishing Fine

Our last game of the regular season was on the road against Froid, a very good team in 2-C that year. They took second with Culbertson first, and both of those teams were pretty good. This was senior night at Froid, and I remember thinking to myself, as I watched the flowers and stuff going on (back to that competitive thing again), "We are going to make you very unhappy on senior night; you shouldn't have scheduled Peerless on senior night." And then we went out and ran all over them, leading 38–19 at half and winning 72–42. One noteworthy thing about that game was that Peerless did not have a single turnover, not one.

So the Froid game concluded the 1979 Panther regular season, and we were 17–3, losing only to Class B power Scobey, and 10–0 in conference. In conference play, we had an average margin of victory of 28 points, and only two Class C teams (Flaxville and Nashua) had scored over 50 points on us the entire season. We were very, very excited about the upcoming District tournament the following week in Plentywood, where we would be shooting for the first District championship in Peerless basketball history, and begin our march to Helena, one more time, in '79 . . .

The Strategic Shift Pays Off

Before we get into the story of Peerless' first ever District championship, I've got to spend a little time talking about our man-to-man defense that year, because it was really our defense that defined us in 1979. After 20 games, we were giving up an average of only 45 points per game, and only two Class C teams had scored over 50 points on us. The fundamental shift in defensive strategy was christened at the beer séance in the Puckett house following that first Opheim game, and it had served us well, both offensively and defensively. Due to the defensive pressure we would put on opposing team's guards in the backcourt, we were able to get out and aggressively force the tempo of the game. We would force a lot of turnovers off the man-to-man full court pressure, and this would start our fast break going the other way, allowing us to run more than we ever had before staying back in that zone.

In any given game, this is his how the 1979 Panthers would match up: I would guard the opposing team's shooting guard, and Bernie would guard the point guard. In some cases, if the point guard was also the guard that scored, I would guard him. Jon would guard the scoring forward, Joel Dighans would guard their center, and Ray Chapman would guard the rebounding, or power forward. This is how we would match up every game. It was incredibly ironic that the run-and-gun Panthers of 1978 would transform into a defense-oriented team in 1979. Don't get me wrong, we still ran—a lot—but our energy was focused on defense, and if you expend a lot of energy on defense it takes a lot out of you. What really symbolized how important our defense had become in 1979 was in our last home game against Lambert, where I was completely focused on defending Nick Vaira. I only scored 12 points in the game, my last home game, and I took maybe six shots from the floor, and it didn't bother me at all. We all took a lot of pride in our defense, and we were winning games because of it.

Another interesting thing about the 1979 team was we were really playing with three true guards every game, with Bernie Wasser in the starting lineup now that Bill Fladager and Roger Trang had graduated. Jon was forced back to guard the forward when we went to the straight man-to-man defense, and because Bernie was really a guard, he and I would defend the guards. This really changed the whole tenor of the court for us, now that Jon was back on defense guarding a forward. In 1978, Jon and I were always out front together, guarding the opposing team's guards, but our defensive set in 1979 would split us up on the court.

Another big difference in 1979 was that I realized, early on, that I needed to rebound more than I ever had before to pick up the load that Bill and Roger had carried the year before. I would always make sure I collapsed into the paint on defense when the shot went up; and Jon would be there too, to help out Joel and Ray. So the irony on defense was, when comparing it to the 1978 team, although we extended our defense full court, in the end we were all back in the paint anyway; the difference was we didn't start there. This meant that many of our fast breaks were started off the dribble when Jon or I got the rebound, whereas the year before, Jon and I would release to the wings off the top of the zone as the shot went up, looking for the outlet pass from Bill, Roger or Joel to start the fast break. And speaking of irony, one of the things you would see a lot in 1979 would be Jon or me getting the rebound and Joel Dighans, our center, racing up the court for a layup on the other end on the fast break, because he was very fast and would beat the opposing team's center down the court. A guard rebounds and the center finishes the fast break on the other end; such was the case with the topsy turvy Panthers of 1979.

The March to Helena Begins

What a difference a year can make! A year earlier, we had finished fourth in the conference, and we'd had to face Outlook, the eventual State champion, in the semi-final game at District. We had lost our two previous semi-final games at District in 1976 and 1977, two tough losses, and then when we were juniors, we had to play the State champions just to escape from District 1-C for the first time in my high school career. As you know, we upset Outlook in that

Ray Chapman shoots in warm ups prior to Westby game at District
as the March to Helena begins in 1979.

game, 75–63, and marched onto State in 1978, finishing third, but it
was rough just getting out of our District. In 1979, we were facing
Westby, the fourth-place team in the conference. We had beaten
them badly both times we played them, 78–38 and 70–37, and this
game would be no different, although they did lead us 12–10 at the
end of the first quarter. Not exactly the bolt out of the blocks we
were looking for as we started our march to Helena in 1979, but by
halftime we led 28–21, and then we pulled away in the second half,
pressuring their guards and holding Westby to seven points in the
third quarter.

Again, it was our defense that allowed us to pull away, and the
game ended with a final score of 66–39, a typical game for the 1979
Panthers, as we had an average margin of victory of 28 points over
Class C teams.

Wow. Is that it? Are you kidding me? One blowout and we're
onto Divisionals? The year before, we have to beat the State
Champion just to escape from 1-C, and now, a year later, all we have

to do is scrimmage one team and we move onto Wolf Point? Cool. This is going to be easy this year. A nice little waltz to State. Ah, maybe not . . .

But unlike a year earlier, when we were so excited to beat Outlook semi-final night and just get out of District, and we'd played poorly against Flaxville in the championship game, this year we were on a mission. We traveled to Plentywood to take the nets and bring the first ever District championship in 46 years home to Peerless. So regardless of who won the second semi-final game that night, whether it was the Outlook Blue Jays or the Flaxville Cardinals (this game would be for the birds), we didn't care. We headed back to the hotel to get some sleep, because whomever it was we were playing the next night, it didn't matter: We were bringing it. Forty-six years. Don't you think it was time?

The Plentywood Pilgrimage

I mentioned previously that beginning in 1975, Dad, Jon and I would make an annual pilgrimage to Helena, the Mecca of Class C high school basketball in Montana, to watch the State C tournament. We always dreamed of playing on that stage in Helena, and that dream would come true, and how! Well, much earlier than that, beginning in about 1965 or so, Dad took us to District every year at Plentywood. I remember watching Gary Nieskens, Terry Puckett and Wallace Fladager play at District for Peerless. It was so exciting to watch those guys play on that court. As a little boy, the Peerless Pep Club seemed so loud and that gym seemed *so* big to me. I also remember how excited all the Peerless kids would be, the pep club and cheerleaders, to go to District, and just generally what a special event it was for everyone involved. I remember my sister Dianne telling me the horror story of how she got chicken pox just days before District—might have even been her senior year in 1967—and she couldn't go to District. She told me how she was trying to makeup on over them on her face so she could still go, and finally Mom and Dad just had to say no way. She was devastated. Not being able to go to District Tournament? You might as well just cancel Christmas.

The first memory I have of the District championship game is when Robin Selvig and Outlook won it in 1970. I remember Robin Selvig taking over the game in the fourth quarter, and I remember the Outlook pep club and cheerleaders on the court following the game, waiting (not so patiently) for the announcer to get around to the first-place trophy, and then just going absolutely berserk when he said, "And now, the first-place trophy, goes to . . . Outlook." KABOOM!

Now, it was our turn to go berserk . . .

District 1-C From 1950–1978

It seemed like every year I went to District tournament it would either be Outlook or Westby (sometimes Medicine Lake) who won the tournament. Why was that? The District 1-C program from 1979, as it did every year, contained a record of the District 1-C finishes since 1949–50, when Class C Basketball was formed in Montana, and District 1-C—as we would come to know it—was formed. Here are the number of District 1-C championships by school from 1950 to 1978:

> Westby 9
> Outlook 7
> Medicine Lake 5
> Antelope 3
> Flaxville 3 (very recent, 1976, '77 and '78)
> Lustre 1
> Opheim 1
> Peerless 0

Opheim and Lustre were also originally in 1-C, but in 1979 both of these teams were in 3-C. Opheim's last year in 1-C was 1973; Lustre left following the 1976 season. The 1971 Opheim team, led by Bob Delay, was probably the best Opheim team I ever saw play, but they were upset by Outlook in the semi-finals at District that year. Only one week prior, Opheim had beaten Outlook by 30 points on their home court. Opheim came back to take third place at District that year, but this was one of those years when only two teams advanced to Divisional, and Outlook lost the championship game to Westby, so Opheim could not challenge. Also, Medicine Lake had competed in Class B for some of these years. Notice the trend of the Daniels County teams, Peerless and Flaxville, not faring so well, except until 1974, when Don Puckett, Dallas and Duke Trangsrud, and Scott Dighans led Peerless to its first ever District championship game appearance and a trip to Divisionals. Peerless took second again in 1975, when Duke, Scott, Jim Chapman, Tom Myers, Steve Miner and the boys upset #1-ranked Westby semi-final night; and then again in 1978, when we upset State champ Outlook semi-final night. Prior to 1976, Flaxville had never played for the championship, but since then they had won it three times in a row, most recently against us the year before in 1978.

The Champion Defends

Well, since Flaxville won the Bird Bowl against Outlook semi-final night 58–44, we were playing Flaxville in a rematch for the District championship. It was as it should be: Peerless vs. Flaxville for the championship. Amazing what a rare occurrence that was in all those years. Our cheerleaders and Flaxville's cheerleaders, in an unusual (but inspiring) display of unity between the two schools, paraded a "Daniels County District 1-C" banner around Plentywood's Fieldhouse prior to the start of the game, not so subtly demonstrating to the Sheridan County folks that basketball supremacy in Northeastern Montana had shifted to the west. Gone were the days of Sheridan County dominance in 1-C. I guess that night the united cheer for Peerless and Flaxville would have been the "Power's in the West" to the Sheridan County folks, although for the remainder of the tournament trail to Helena, it would be the "Power's in the East."

So now we play Flaxville once again, District Champion for the last three years. We had beaten Flaxville both times in conference during the season, most recently clinching our first ever Conference

"Daniels County District 1-C" banner unveiled by Peerless and Flaxville cheerleaders at District 1-C championship, 1979.

championship against them only two weeks earlier, 57–47 at Flaxville. We were sky high for this game, and I remember I couldn't wait to get on the court to play. The Plentywood Fieldhouse was rocking too, as both Peerless and Flaxville fans were anticipating another tenacious matchup between these two rivals—this time on the District championship stage—the first of what would be three tournament championship games between these two rivals. And as the players for the two teams ran out onto the court to the familiar "Go Cards Go!" and "Go Panthers Go!" chants, the level of intensity and energy in the fieldhouse was rising ever higher, cresting only as 5'11" Joel Dighans and 6'7" Kevin Hatfield sprang upward to gain possession of the opening tip . . .

As the first couple minutes of the championship game unfolded, the pace, emotion and intensity of the game was furious; and, as Flaxville came out and scored the first four points of the game, I learned something very quickly: This was not the same team we had played just two weeks earlier in Flaxville. They were playing on a much higher level, both emotionally and physically. Don't forget: This team was defending a championship they had won for three

Jon Puckett fights for the ball with David Weltikol and Mike Safty.
Peerless vs. Flaxville, District 1-C championship, 1979.

straight years, and this was the fourth consecutive District championship game for senior Kevin Hatfield, and he had won the previous three. So, although we had beaten Flaxville three times in a row, beginning with the challenge game to go to State the previous year, and culminating at Flaxville when we clinched the conference championship just two weeks earlier, this was their championship to defend, and we were trying to take it away from them.

One of the beautiful things about good competition is that it forces you to take your game up to another level, both as a team and individually. And early on in that Flaxville game, all of us realized that if we were going to win the first District championship in our school's 46-year history, we were going to have to hike our game up to another level, or two, or three . . . Flaxville was playing inspired basketball, and we knew it, we could feel it. I remember when I made the first basket for our team in that game, the Peerless crowd just erupted. I can't remember them being any louder for any basket our team made, with the exception of Jon's shot with four seconds left against Wibaux in the State consolation game the previous year. They were ready to rock, and were waiting for that first basket to go down.

Flaxville took the lead at the end of the first quarter, 17–11; then, they scored the first two points of the second quarter to go up

19–11. I remember that score because we had trailed Outlook by the same score in the 2nd quarter of the semi-final game the previous year. This was not a comfortable position for us to be in. We had not trailed like this in a game since we played Scobey before Christmas, and the noise of Flaxville's crowd was really starting to swell. There was no need to panic, of course—it was still early—but we needed to pick it up here a little bit.

We did. And again, it was our man-to-man defense that did it, allowing us to fight back and take the lead 27–25 at halftime. We only allowed Flaxville to score six points the remainder of that quarter, and we managed to run our offense well enough against Flaxville's sticky, collapsing man-to-man defense to score 16 ourselves; we basically went on a 16–6 run to end half. But we were in a half court game with Flaxville in the first half, a style of play that was very dangerous to play against this team, and we needed to break out and run in the second half and open up the court, which we would do, like we had never done before . . .

In the locker room at halftime, Coach Niccum was animated and intense as he always was. He was happy with our defense; we had really tightened it up in the second quarter. But our offense was struggling. In particular, Jon was having a hard time getting into the game offensively. Whenever this would happen, whenever either Jon or I struggled offensively in the first half, Niccum would call a set play to open the second half where one of us (whichever twin was struggling) would come off a screen on the baseline to get a good look at the basket in the hopes that a good look would break us into the game offensively. We ran that play in the second half for Jon, and he made the basket. From that point on, Jon was back in the game offensively. Niccum was a great coach that way; he knew when to call a certain play to get things going, just like Coach Shaffer had before him. We were so lucky to have the coaching we did at Peerless.

The Run

The way we had beaten Flaxville the previous three games was to go on quick scoring spurts brought about by our press and ensuing fast break. Usually a quick 8–0 or 10–0 run would catapult us into the lead, and then we would hold serve from that point on, and towards end of the game we would play a little ball control (we could be methodical too) and Flaxville would have to foul us. We were an excellent free throw shooting team and would often win close games by making our free throws in the end. In the challenge game at Divisionals in 1978, our scoring burst (actually it was more like an eruption that game) came in the fourth quarter, where we outscored Flaxville 29–16. In the first game at Peerless in 1979, that flurry of points against them came in the 2nd quarter, where we forced numerous turnovers off our pressure defense and converted them into fast-break baskets to outscore them 25–8 in the quarter. At Flaxville, where we clinched the conference championship, we went on a 6–0 run at the end of the third quarter, brought about again by our pressure defense, breaking open a close game and taking a 40–29 lead going into the fourth quarter.

Would that all-important spurt come against Flaxville in the championship game? Oh yes it would!

This time, the run would come late in the third quarter. In 1979, after the fundamental shift in defensive strategy was sealed at the late-night beer séance, with my dad and Coach Niccum at the Puckett house following our first game against Opheim, we would continuously pressure the ball with our man-to-man press, and all it took was one lapse by the opposing team's guards, one mistake, and we would get a steal and be gone the other way for a layup. Then we would feed off of that steal and layup to get another, and then another, and in a matter of seconds we could turn a close game into a 10-point lead for the Panthers. This is why it was the right decision to shift to the man-to-man defense that year; we never could have had those scoring bursts if we were all tucked neatly back in that zone the whole game.

So in the third quarter, our man-to-man press broke through

once again, and in a furious attack, we rallied to light up the scoreboard with eight consecutive points, breaking the game open to take
a 45–35 lead going into the fourth quarter. I remember after I made
a layup off a fast break at the end of the rally, Flaxville called a
timeout to stop the bleeding. I had never been so pumped up in all
my life. It was pure adrenaline. After the timeout was called and we
all sprinted back to the huddle Niccum was like, "Hey, settle down,
there's a lot of game left to play, this isn't over!" He then said,
"What a show you guys are putting on!" We knew it wasn't over, but
we also knew that we had just got that quick scoring spurt we always
needed to beat Flaxville and we had the momentum going into the
fourth quarter. We were getting close, but not there yet . . .

Forty-Six Years

Coming out to start the fourth quarter, we were eight minutes away
from the first District championship in our school's history, but it
was *way* too early to start thinking about that. We had all played
enough basketball to know that this game was far from over, but we
also knew that we had just opened the game up with that run in the
third quarter, and we had Flaxville on the ropes. As the fourth
quarter progressed, minute by minute, possession by possession, we
were holding serve with Flaxville. Our ten-point lead was safe, and
we gradually began to expand on it. Less than four minutes left and
our lead was expanding! Don't let up! Bring it on home! The clock
continued to wind down, three minutes, and then, we started to take
the air out of the ball a little bit. Flaxville had to start fouling. We
could start to taste it. Just need to make those free throws, Panthers!
Swish. Swish. Swish. One after another, we made our free throws,
and the lead steadily expanded, even as the time on the clock
continued to tick down. The Panthers sank 17 of 19 free throws in
the game, and the lead expanded all the way up to 18 points In the
end, the District championship game turned into a rout, 65–47!

Forty-six years! F.R. Puckett establishes PHS in 1932–33, and 46
years later the Peerless Panthers are crowned District Champions for
the first time in the school's history! Ten! Nine! Eight! Seven! Six!

Five! Four! Three! Two! One! The Peerless Panthers are District Champions! The hardware and nets are coming to Peerless! A perfect 10–0 Conference record and now the Panthers sweep through the District Tournament! Ronnie Jones, fire up the bus, the Peerless Panthers are coming to Wolf Point!

GAME AND TOURNAMENT NOTES

Peerless made 17–19 free throws in the game . . . Peerless outscored Flaxville 38–22 in the second half . . . Joe Puckett led the Panthers with 28 points . . . Doug Selvig of Outlook became the fifth son of Roald and Agnes Selvig to be named to the District 1-C All-Tourney team, following Ken, Robin, Randy, and Dave . . . In a surefire sign of Sheridan County favoritism—which Daniels County had fallen prey to for thirty years—the Outlook cheerleaders won the cheerleading trophy over both Peerless and Flaxville, who would ultimately finish 1–2 in the state . . .

Jon Puckett takes the nets following Peerless' victory over Flaxville in the District 1-C championship, 1979.

Peerless co-captains (from left) Ray Chapman, Jon and Joe Puckett
receive first ever District 1-C championship trophy for Peerless, 1979.

The Ceiling

Every team has a ceiling, a level at which they cannot possibly take
their game any higher. In the District championship game against
Flaxville, the 1979 Peerless Panthers had reached their ceiling. You
would not see this team play any better than they did in the second
half against Flaxville in the District Tourney. Everything we had
worked for all season came together: Our perimeter shooting,
pressure man-to-man defense, fast break, rebounding, free throws,
everything. We brought the best game we possibly could to Flaxville
that night to win our school's first ever District championship. We
had peaked. Didn't know it at the time, but we had. Unfortunately
for us, Coach Bakken and Flaxville were still improving, still
adapting and still learning how to play us better, and unfortunately
this would not be the last time we would face this team. Unfortunately . . .

Almost Played Them All

When I saw the bracket for Divisionals, we were scheduled to play Savage. I was excited to play Savage for a reason you might find amusing: I had never played Savage before. They were one of only two teams left in the East C Division I had never played, and I wanted to play every team in the East Division. Here are the teams I had played in the East Division (outside of 1-C) in my high school career, with our record against those teams in parenthesis:

District 2-C:
> Froid Cardinals (1–0)
> Bainville Bulldogs(1–0)
> Culbertson Cowboys (3–0)
> Lambert Lions (1–0)
> Richey Royals(1–0)
> Brockton Warriors(2–0)
> Savage Warriors (1–0)

District 3-C
> Nashua Porkies (1–0)
> Lustre Lions (1–0)
> Saco Panthers (1–0)
> Hinsdale Red Raiders(2–0)
> Whitewater Penguins (1–0)
> Frazer Bearcubs (1–0)
> Opheim Vikings (3–3)

So, the only team I did not play from the Eastern C Division in high school was the Dodson Coyotes.

Interestingly, I played against two teams from outside the Eastern C Division during the regular season. In my freshman year, before Christmas, in 1975, we played Hingham and Rudyard from the Northern Division (District 9-C) at the Rudyard Invitational Tournament in December. Joplin was there too. This was before they were known as Joplin-Inverness. So we travel 260 miles (six hours) to play an incredibly talented and *huge* Hingham team in the first game. They beat us badly, by 20 points. Hingham had a very good team and a huge frontline. Couldn't believe we drove all that way to play them and then get rocked by 20. I remember hearing some of the 9-C fans in the crowd saying to us as we left the court, "Man, that's a pretty long way to travel just to get your asses kicked." They were all wondering what we were doing there. We were wondering that too. That Hingham team would go onto take third place at State that year, defeating a previously undefeated Manhattan Christian team not once, but two times in the tournament. This was the same year Flaxville won the State tournament for the first time, the year Kevin Hatfield was a freshman. Hingham had a really good team, with Mike Farnik at forward and Brian Patrick at center. In the consolation game, we played host Rudyard and destroyed them by almost 30 points. This was the only time in high school I won the last game before Christmas, and this was also the year I got new 8-track tape player from Santa Claus, the year I really didn't need it. The annual PCIT started the following year, and we lost the championship game of the PCIT my sophomore, junior and senior years. This was also the only time Peerless played a regular season game against a Class C team from outside of the Eastern Division.

Marching On

I was glad we were going back to play Divisionals at Wolf Point, rather than Glasgow. We had picked up a few fans in Wolf Point the previous year and I was hoping they might come back to watch us play. And they did. Every little bit helps; I was always thinking that way. I knew how much the crowd had helped us the year before at both Wolf Point and Helena, *especially* at Helena, so it was an advantage for us playing at Wolf Point again. Plus, the last time I had played on that court was against Flaxville in the challenge game the previous year, when our lifelong dream of making it to State would come true for all of us. Let's just say that court had special memories for me.

Savage was the third seed from 2-C. We were anxious to get on the court at Divisionals and get on with the march to Helena, but we would have to wait; the first game of the tournament, Opheim vs. Culbertson, went into overtime in one of the wildest endings to a game I'd ever seen. We were up on the court from the locker room, ready to run onto the court to warm up for our game, so I got to see the end of the game. Opheim had the ball and a two-point lead with just a few seconds left, when Bobby Damm, an excellent guard from Culbertson, intercepted a pass, shot the ball, and then got fouled on the shot at the buzzer. So, as time had expired, he went to the line by himself to shoot two free throws to tie the game. Well, he shoots the first free throw and I swear it danced on the rim for about ten seconds and hung there, and then the ball just finally gave up and fell through the net, tired of fighting with the rim any longer. He walked off the line, turned his back on the basket, and then came back to shoot the second one. This time, the ball hit the heel of the rim and bounced about six feet straight up in the air, and then came back down cleanly through the net to send the game into overtime! So we went back into the locker room because this game was going to go on for another three minutes! Opheim ended up winning the game in overtime, so we were going to play them the next night, in what would be the closest, most difficult, insanely intense game I ever played in, where we would come within a few harrowing seconds of not returning to State in 1979.

But first we had to beat Savage, and that would prove to be no problem at all. They reminded me of Bainville—very athletic, physical, tough, but not especially gifted basketball players. I think they had a good football program as well. We were able to run on them at will and pester their guards, opening up a 35–20 halftime lead and then blowing them out in the end 75–43. It was a typical game for us against non-1-C opponents: A rout. It was also nice to have a game like that at Divisionals, because we could just relax late in the third quarter and early in the fourth quarter, just have some fun on the court, run and run, kind of like a scrimmage back home in the Peerless gym.

So, after three games on the tournament trail in 1979, we were

beating opponents by an average of 25 points a game, and everything was going according to plan: Sweep through the tournaments
and don't let anyone get in our way. Well, the next night Opheim—
the team that gave us fits our first game of the year—would once
again put a scare into the Panthers, this time with much higher
stakes on the line than a birth in the Nashua Invitational Tournament championship game in November. This time, a trip to State
was very well on the line, and it would be close, oh so close . . .

In the four seasons I played in high school, our record against
non-1-C teams was 17–3, with all three losses coming to Opheim.
We had lost to them three times my sophomore year when Niccum
was coaching them. Now, I was a senior, and we were one game
away from a repeat trip to the Divisional championship game, with
only Loren E. Baker's Opheim team in our way. Loren E. Baker
would have a little trick up his sleeve that he had been concealing
since our first game against them in the Nashua tournament in
November. It was now time to for him to unveil that trick . . .

The Triangle and Two

This is a game that if you talk to any 1979 Panther they'll probably
tell you they still have nightmares about it. We came very close to
getting upset by Opheim that night and most likely not returning to
State our senior year. Flaxville was playing very well and probably
would have beat Opheim in the championship game, not allowing us
to challenge, if we had even gotten that far. A lot of factors came
together in that game to make it the "Perfect Storm" for an upset.
Dad would later refer to that game as the "Shitstorm on Friday night
at Wolf Point," and it was.

One of the biggest obstacles we faced in that game was Loren
Baker's coaching. He had prepared his team very well against us, to
say the least, and inspired them to play at a peak level that entire
game. He brought his team out in the dreaded triangle and two
defense. They stuck with it the entire game, and just gave us fits with
it. Later on, in 1995, Joel and Jerod Nieskens would see this same
defensive set in the State championship game against Belt, and it

gave them fits as well. It is the perfect solution to shutdown a team with two guards who can both shoot and penetrate, like Joe and Jon Puckett for the 1979 Panthers and Joel and Jerod Nieskens for the 1995 Panthers.

It was the strangest thing I'd seen all year. Jon and I were bringing the ball up the court for the first time against Opheim and their guards were pressing us. What? You're going to press us? We had never seen that before in either 1978 or 1979, and at first I was like, "Yeah, bring it on, we're going to dribble through you and shoot layups all night, and you'll be out of this before the end of the first quarter." But that didn't happen. It was only their guards that were pressuring us, actually shadowing us full court, everywhere on the court. Their front line of 6'6" Norm Dyrland, 6'3" Rick Maus, and 6'3" Brent Lawrence were waiting for us back in the paint in a triangle zone, one on the high post and two on the block. If we beat their guards on the dribble there was a zone waiting for us on the other end, so it didn't matter—we couldn't dribble penetrate all the way to the basket. I don't think Jon or I had a layup the entire game. This is why the triangle and two is such a good defense to stop two players who share both the shooting and dribbling burden for a team: It is designed to shutdown *both* the dribble penetration *and* the shots, combining the principles of both a man-to-man defense and a zone defense in the same set. It worked to perfection for Opheim against us. It was so difficult for Jon and me to shake our defenders because Opheim rotated four guards against us on defense and they were always fresh. The guy that was defending Jon and me would turn his back on the ball, not playing the ball at all, and only shadow Jon and me man-to-man the whole length of the court, following us wherever we went.

So where is the triangle and two weak? Well, we had never seen it before this game; we didn't expect it and we couldn't solve the riddle during the game. None of us saw it coming—including our coaching staff—and we weren't able to make any adjustments that worked. It was surprising that Jon and I didn't see more triangle twos our senior year, because of how well it worked for Opheim in this game. But we would see it again at State, and man did we ever dismantle it there—just shredded it after Niccum figured out how to beat it in practice those two weeks before State. More on that later.

Since Opheim was in the triangle and two (a man-to-man on two people and a zone on the other three) do you run your passing game offense or your zone offense? We ran our zone offense most of the time and that, I believe, was a mistake, because it was very difficult for Jon and I to get shots off without any screens being set, and in our zone offense we didn't set any screens. Bernie, Joel and Ray had to step up and shoot more than they normally did because the defense not only limited how many shots Jon and I could take, but it also limited the number of times we could even touch the ball. Jon and I shot 15–23 from the floor that game, but had to struggle for every shot, and had a hand in our face every shot. The triangle and two forces the other team to beat you with the other three players, and unfortunately in this game Joel, Ray and Bernie and the rest of the team did not have good games offensively, and collectively shot 9–28 from the floor. It was just one of those games where it seemed like they put a lid on the basket and they couldn't buy a bucket, although they had good looks. As the game progressed, and the score stayed close, the lid over the basket seemed to get larger and larger . . .

Another thing Opheim did was force us into a half court game, which is what Flaxville was able to do whenever they were successful against us. Also, Opheim's guards (Randy Stolen, Darrell Walstad, Kevin St. John, who coached Chester against the 1995 Panthers, and Craig Ross) could handle our pressure, and we never could break out and run that game. Opheim's guards were very conservative and would stay back on defense, and Randy Stolen did a good job of handling the ball so we didn't force many turnovers. It became apparent as the game wore on that this was going to be a hard fight and we weren't ever going to get that spurt of points we would usually get to break games open. We couldn't shake them. The game started to get very frustrating for us as Opheim hung within two to four points the entire game . . . we all started to get a little tight, playing not to lose, something that I had never experienced before, and it was not a lot of fun. It was not our style of ball to play tentatively, but that's what was happening to us and we didn't know what to do about it.

Clang!

We never trailed the entire game in regulation, and we led at the end of the first quarter, 12–10; 25–22 halftime and 38–36 at the end of the third quarter. The fourth quarter was as intense a quarter as I ever played in. We were attacking the basket that Opheim's bench was on, and Loren Baker was running up and down the side of the court yelling at his team every time we were on offense. He was so animated, you could see him out of the corner of your eye, could hear him shouting, "FIGHT 'EM TIL THE LAST SECOND, FIGHT 'EM TIL THE LAST SECOND." It was as if he was on the court with his team, guarding Jon and me along with his other two guards. It was like a triangle and three, with Loren on the court with his team!

With about a minute left, we managed to inch the lead up to four points, and then Loren Baker told his team to start to fouling us because we were in a four corners. He intentionally fouled Ray Chapman to send Ray to the line for two free throws. This was a lot of pressure to put on a kid, Loren told his team to foul Ray when Ray didn't even have the ball. Ray missed both free throws and Opheim came down and scored, and the next possession down the court he intentionally fouled Ray *again*. I had never seen that before in my entire career. Loren was coaching to win that game in every way he could. The thing is, Ray was a decent free throw shooter, as coming into that game, he had made 26–38 free throws for almost 70%. That's a decent free throw shooter, especially for high school. In fact, Ray was the third-best free throw shooter on our team, behind Jon and me. Joel Dighans did not shoot that well from the line; neither did Bernie Wasser. So Loren wasn't playing the percentages. He must have got it in his head he was going to foul Ray, which he did and it just happened to work for him. Ray missed the second two free throws as well, then with about 20 seconds left, Opheim tied the game at 49 on a free throw.

Coach Niccum called a timeout to setup a final shot. The play he called was either for Jon or me to take the ball on the dribble to the basket, then look for the shot or pass to an open teammate. After play resumed, somehow I got the ball on the dribble just to the right of the key with two seconds left. The whistle blew and a foul was called! I was going to the line to shoot a one-and-one free throw to send us to State! Loren Baker called a timeout to freeze me, of course, and I remember when I came back out onto the court I didn't feel right. Prior to that game, I had made 67–74 free throws that year for 90%, but earlier in the game, I had missed two free throws in a row and that had never happened to me the entire year. I was thinking about that when I came to the line at the end of the game. It was like in that game I was in a slump shooting free throws; my mechanics just didn't feel right. Normally a good free throw shooter will only miss long or short, but earlier in that game I had missed to the side, and I couldn't explain it, it was just one of those nights.

But after all of this, I had the opportunity in the last moments of the game to end it all at the free throw line, and I was a 90% free throw shooter. So I came up to the line to shoot and I wasn't feeling right at all. I took the ball and go through my routine, shoot the free throw and . . . CLANG! I mean the mother of all bricks hits that basket and shakes the gym. Shaq has shot better balls than that. I knew it was off the moment it left my hand; it didn't have a chance.

And now, after Opheim had never the led the entire game, we were headed to overtime to decide who would move on to play in the championship game the next night, and most likely advance to the State tournament in Helena . . .

Down and Then Up Again

Running out onto to the court for overtime was not a good feeling. We had led the entire game, up until the final 20 seconds. We had missed five straight free throws in the final minute. And if we had only made one of those free throws, we would not have been in overtime. Normally, we won games with our free throw shooting, but now, ironically, we were faced with the possibility of losing one because of it. Opheim's crowd had become very loud, sensing that an upset might be coming in overtime, and now *we* were the team that would get upset, unlike the year before when we were always the underdog. It was a completely different feeling. Psychologically, it was difficult not to start thinking that somehow we were snake bit in that game, and that it was headed for a tragic ending . . .

But that didn't happen. Somehow, someway, all five of us reached deep down inside, putting the adversity of the last minute of regulation behind us and focusing on the overtime. It was tense, each possession was critical, as the score was tied, and both teams each extremely deliberate and very careful to get a good shot, had two, maybe three possessions in the extra period. Naturally, Opheim stayed in the triangle and two on defense, as the 49 points they had held us to in regulation was our second-lowest point total of the season (Scobey had held us to 46), and it was 20 points below our average. On offense, Opheim patiently passed the ball around to get it to their 6'6" center Norm Dyrland or 6'3" forward Ricky Maus, who between them scored 41 of Opheim's 51 points in the game.

After a couple possessions in overtime, the score remained tied at 49. We had possession of the ball and Jon was fouled. We were in the bonus, so Jon was shooting one and one. I remember standing at half court thinking, "Come on Jon, you can do it, you've got to be the one to break us out of this free throw jinx of five misses in a row." And he did! Swish! 50–49. He shot the second free throw and . . . misses! So now Opheim had the ball with a chance to take the lead. They were very deliberate, patiently worked the ball around the perimeter, looked for the chance to get the ball inside. The clock ticked down to under a minute, maybe about 40 seconds and Opheim was still passing the ball around to get it inside and then Opheim got the ball on the post, and the shot was made! Opheim had the lead with maybe 30 seconds left in overtime! Their crowd was going berserk as the upset was in the making!

It now seemed like everything was crashing down all around us. This wasn't the script we had planned on to make it to State. Up to that game, we had blown teams out in the tournament by an average of 25 points, and we had never trailed in the second half of a game since we had played Scobey before Christmas. Now we were within seconds of losing in the semi-finals at Divisional and perhaps not making it to State our senior year. We were out of timeouts, so Niccum couldn't call a timeout to setup a play. It was probably just as well. I remember bringing the ball up the court on the dribble; both Opheim and Peerless crowds were on their feet, and I actually took a deep breath as I was dribbling and very quickly said a little prayer to calm myself: "Just take your time, there's plenty of time left, you don't have to panic, get a good shot off." One of Opheim's guards was shadowing me on the dribble, but always giving me a little room so that I couldn't dribble by him to the basket. I was on the right side of the court, slowing coming up it, taking my time, and I could see that there was a way to get a shot off against this guy, without a screen. I remembered all of the one-on-one games Jon and I had played. We always shot off the dribble against each other because we knew each other's moves so well that we couldn't dribble past to the basket. So I dribbled to the top of the key on the right side, I accelerated my dribble to the right to push the defender back just a little, and then pulled up quickly and spun in the air to square to the basket and let fly an 18-footer. Unlike the free throw I had shot with two seconds left in regulation, this shot felt good. It was headed straight for the bottom of the net. It was almost the same exact shot Jon had made against Wibaux the year before in the consolation game at State. Would it have the same result? Arching down and . . . Swish! Timeout Opheim! Only seconds left! We all ran back to the huddle feeling pumped. I remember Jon came right up to my face and yelled, "NICE SHOT JOEY!" almost knocking me over, just like he had done in the challenge game against Flaxville the year before. Now it was 52–51 Peerless, and in just a matter of seconds we had recaptured the precious lead.

A Close Call

After the timeout, we knew Opheim was going to come out and try to get the ball inside. We were playing a collapsing man-to-man defense to prevent that from happening, but with about 20 seconds left, somehow Norm Dyrland got the ball on the low post clear from Joel Dighans, he had a wide open lane to the basket that a truck could drive through. I thought, "Oh my God. How did that happen!" as he took a dribble toward the basket. But from his position at forward, Jon slid over in front of him to take the charge and he got good position; they made contact, Jon flew back into the wall, and Dyrland followed through with the layup. Whistle! Foul on the play! Who was the foul going to be on? It looked like Jon had good position, but we didn't know which way the call was going to go! Then, referee Myron Gackle of Circle, refereeing with his partner Bob Erickson, stepped out to the side of the key and put his hand behind his head and pointed in the direction of Peerless! Offensive foul on Dyrland! Oh, you can't imagine the roar that came up from the crowd at that point, Peerless in jubilation and Opheim in frustration.

Jon either shot free throws off that charging call, or on our next possession he was fouled, I'm not sure which. In either event, he was at the free throw line again, this time with a chance to ice it if he hit both ends of the one-and-one. Come on Jon, two free throws and we get the hell out of this mess. The first one arched up and . . . Swish! 53–51. Jon let out a deep sigh and stepped off the line, came back up, shot the second free throw and . . . Swish again! Grace under pressure! Timeout Opheim! The score was now 54–51 Peerless, with only a few precious seconds remaining.

Opheim came down and missed a quick shot, and the ball went out of bounds on us. There were only a few seconds left in the game at that point. Loren Baker called another timeout and then sent his team back onto the court. We pulled everyone back to half court, didn't even want to get close to those guys to foul, just needed to let them inbound and shoot the layup and the game was over. So Loren Baker, coaching that game right up until the last second, had one guy inbound and one guy on the block, then positioned his other players to quickly grab and intentionally foul us after they inbounded and made the basket. It was an odd thing to see five Panthers at half court watching two Vikings under the basket to end that wild game.

I was yelling at everyone, "GET AWAY FROM THEM BECAUSE THEY'RE GOING TO FOUL YOU AFTER THEY SHOOT! MOVE BACK!" It was intense right up to the last second. The shot was missed, but they still tried to grab us to foul as the shot harmlessly dribbled off the rim and the buzzer sounded, ending the most traumatic game any of us had ever played. But, ugly as it was, somehow, someway, we found a way to win that game, 54–51 in overtime.

The Quiet Locker Room

So we had just survived a scare, dodged a bullet, however you want to put it. Actually, for me it was more like a near-death experience. The strange thing was, we had just won a close semi-final game at Divisionals and were headed to the Divisional championship game for the second year in a row, and, considering how well Opheim was playing, maybe we had even clinched a berth into the State tournament as well (turns out we had, as Opheim would win the consolation). But we walked off the court almost as if we had lost the game, relieved but not jubilant. In the locker room, twelve Panthers sat on the bench in the locker room looking down at the floor, in shock. There was no celebration. We hadn't won the game; we had avoided losing, and that was the difference. We continued to sit there, saying nothing. Even Coach Niccum, who was never at a loss for words, didn't say anything. We sat there and took deep breaths, maybe looking up at each other occasionally. You literally could have heard a pin drop in that locker room. Bruce Fladager was in there with us, as he always was after big wins; he would come down to the locker room, and I would look for him because it was comforting to see him there, it meant we had won the game and we would talk a little bit about the game and share in the celebration. But there was no celebration in that locker room. Finally, after what seemed like several minutes, Bruce Fladager threw his arms up in the air and said to all of us in frustration, "Well, you won!" He couldn't understand why we were so down, you know, like what's wrong with you guys? After Bruce said that, we started to stir around a little bit and come back to life, get ready to shower. It was okay, we were moving on, and by the time we got back into the bleachers to watch the Flaxville-Outlook semi-final game, we were all breathing a lot easier. It was finally sinking in that we had actually survived the scare and won the game; we had come through it, and we were going to be playing for the Divisional championship game.

Breathing Easier

As the Outlook-Flaxville semi-final game progressed, we started to talk to each other and laugh and smile a little bit and share in that big win we had just had. It was great. We had come very close to getting knocked off, but, in the end, we came through as champions. It felt awesome sitting next to my teammates, relaxing and enjoying the sweet feeling of victory. I looked up across the court at Steve Keller, assistant coach for Opheim, and I could see him replaying the game in his head. Recognizing that they had come so close to upsetting us, he put his head in his hands and looked down. That same night, in Miles City, his younger brother Jeff would lead Custer to a win in the Southern Divisional semi-final game against Wibaux (remember them?), and Custer would go on to win the Southern Divisional. Since we would lose to Flaxville in the championship game the next night, we would be playing the number-one seed from the South, Custer, in the first game of the State tournament. Do you think we might see the triangle and two against Custer in Helena?

An Early Poem

After this traumatic free throw-shooting experience for me, I think it's a good time to share with you a poem I wrote about basketball when I was in fourth, maybe fifth grade. Yes, the first poem I ever wrote was about basketball. My mom saved it and put it in my scrapbook, the scrapbook she meticulously maintained for all of the years I played basketball at Peerless.

It seems at a very early age I had captured the fact that it's much easier to shoot while you're dribbling and moving than it is to stand there at the free throw line with everyone watching you. The Opheim game at divisional proved to be a perfect demonstration of this for me, as I missed the free throw at the end of regulation but made the basket off the dribble at the end of overtime. Here it is ...

Basketball
by Joey Puckett

When a person plays basketball it is a good feeling,
To dribble past a defender and shoot for the weaving.
It's so thrilling to see the ball hit the hoop and fall through,
And I assure you, everybody on your team will like you.
But, it's not too thrilling to let a defender
Steal the ball from you and go in for a layup.
Then, you will say, "I'm sorry guys," and they'll say, "Shut up!"
The most tense part is a free throw when you walk up to the line,
You're so tense you can feel a shiver run down your spine.
And when the ball is in the air, you're full of despair.
But when the game is over and you win,
Happiness falls over you.
But when you lose you feel ashamed
But after all, it's only a game.

Go Dog Go

I was so keyed up that night at the hotel, I couldn't sleep at all. I was totally hyped. My eyes were wide open, looking around. I was thinking about the game and just how close we'd come to getting knocked off. Whenever I read the book *Go Dog Go!* to my kids, I always chuckle to myself when I get to that page where it's at night and all of dogs are sleeping before the big party the next day— except for one who's laying there with his eyes wide open, stressed out. That would be me that night in Wolf Point. Finally, at about 4:30 in the morning, I got up and drank about a half a bottle of Nyquil (I had a cold) just so I could get some sleep before we got up for breakfast the next morning.

The Clang Echoes

On Saturday afternoon, after we had played the game from hell Friday night, barely escaping what would have been a disastrous scenario, trying to come back through the back door to challenge Flaxville (yes, it would have been Flaxville, and only if Opheim had beaten them), what did we do to relax before the championship game? Niccum had us all come up to his hotel room, all twelve of us. He talked to us about the Opheim game, what we did wrong, and then *he put the tape of the Opheim game in the VCR and played the entire game so we could relive the horror all over again. Oh my God!* And you know what, even though there was no audio on the VHS, I swear I could actually hear the CLANG sound of that brick I shot from the free throw line with two seconds left in regulation. The mood of the team was not good; we were down. I think it would have been better to just go bowling or something, get our minds off the game; that is exactly what we needed at that point.

Going Dancing Again!

Opheim and Culbertson both won the morning games; Culbertson knocked out Doug Selvig and Outlook and Opheim beat Froid. That same Outlook team would win State the following year in 1980, beating the same Opheim team that was playing for the consolation. In 1979, both of those teams had mostly juniors playing, and they would be tough to beat the following year, when it would be another 1–2 finish for the East at State, the last year that State would be held in Helena.

The consolation game was extremely close, just as it had been when Opheim and Culbertson played overtime the first game of the tournament. We were getting periodic updates in the locker room, tracking the score as the game progressed. We were going to the Big Dance again if Opheim won, as they could not challenge us. So we were big Opheim fans that night, just as they would be rooting for us hard against Flaxville in the championship game. When it got into the last minute, it was a one-point game, and I was like, "Come on

Opheim!" In the end, Opheim pulled out another nail-biter 58–57, sending the Panthers to State. Culbertson and Opheim, two very good teams, finished the season 20–6 and 22–6, respectively.

So we were running onto the court knowing we were headed to State again! Only 24 hours earlier we were in the fight for our lives just to stave off that upset, and now *we were in!* What a fantastic feeling! We're already in the Dance *before* we even play the game! Wow! I felt like my feet couldn't even touch the floor; we were going back to Helena with no pressure on us to win that championship game. When we were shooting layups in our pre-game warm up, I remember Kevin Ordahl, a very fine guard from Outlook, walking on the sidelines; he shook my hand and congratulated me on making it back to State. I was springing so high on layups and my shot felt so good it was like I couldn't miss. In warm ups, I told Jon "I feel great, get me the ball tonight." Two hours of sleep and an overtime game the night before, and I felt better than I ever had warming up before a game. Just goes to show you how much emotion can transfer into physical energy. I was pumped!

According to Plan

So we ran out onto the court to start the game, gunning for Peerless' first ever Divisional championship, playing Flaxville for the fourth time that season. Everything was still going according to plan. We came out strong, and played very well in the first half. I felt like I couldn't miss; I was lighting it up from all over the court. We led 14–10 at the end of the first quarter, and I hit a shot from the baseline with just seconds left before halftime to put us ahead 28–20. After I made that shot, the Flaxville player guarding me retrieved the ball and shoved it into my gut as I was running off the court. I turned around and glared at him as he ran off the court. The rivalry was flaring up. If the ref had seen it there would have been a technical called, but he didn't. Later on in the game, the ref would see a similar incident where he would call a technical foul, but not this time.

Obviously, we were playing very well defensively, holding Flaxville to a lower point-total at halftime (20) than we had done in our previous three games against them that year. Joel Dighans was shutting Hatfield down (Hatfield would only score nine points in the game), and our defense was strong all the way around. We sprinted into the locker room carrying a strong eight-point lead with us, and were 16 minutes away from our school's first ever Divisional championship and the #1 seed from the East at State. We didn't know at the time that it would be 16 years later before the Peerless Panthers would reach that milestone, when the 1995 Panthers, led by another brother tandem, Jerod and Joel Nieskens, defeated the Medicine Lake Honkers for Peerless' first (and only) Divisional championship!

The problem at halftime against Flaxville was our offense. Of our 28 points, I had scored 18 of them, so we didn't have that balance we normally had. My shots were coming off the normal offensive pattern we had (Flaxville always played us straight man-to-man), and I wasn't shooting any more than I normally did, nor was I going one-on-one—I just wasn't missing. But as a team we were struggling offensively, and this would catch up with us in the second half, where we would score only 24 points.

The Plan Unravels

To start the second half, Flaxville came out and scored the first eight points. Now it was their turn to go on a run, like we normally did. They were on fire, like a new team. We could not seem to find the basket, I came down and hit another shot on the baseline to put us back up by two, and the game pretty much seesawed back and forth at two points until the end of the third quarter, when the game was tied at 37.

In that third quarter, Flaxville had turned a corner. I think they started to believe they could actually beat us again; in the previous three games we had played against them, we had strong leads going into the fourth quarter, but not this time. I remembered back to the District championship; we were leading by 18 points late in the game, I was standing on the free throw line, and a Flaxville player said to me, "You guys are good but we're going to getcha." Couldn't believe he could actually talk trash in that situation! Flaxville had the momentum and had outscored us by eight points in the quarter. Eight minutes to go and it was all even. The "Go Panthers Go!" and "Go Cards Go!" cheers were deafening again, but the "Go Panthers Go!" cheer was stronger, aided by our newest friend, Opheim, who needed us to beat Flaxville to challenge on Monday night.

It was late in the third quarter when Flaxville got the technical foul called on them. It was a jump ball at center court, and I was on the jump circle next to the Flaxville player. He plopped his foot on top of mine on the circle, so I couldn't move my foot. The ref saw it and called a technical. So I went to the line to shoot the technical. I was at the line by myself, on the same end of the court I shot the brick the night before, and I heard "choke, choke" chants coming out of the Flaxville crowd, calling attention to the night before when I missed that critical free throw against Opheim. I calmly swished the technical foul shot, and shot 9–9 from the line against Flaxville that night from the free throw line. Back to myself again there. About midway through the fourth quarter, or it might have been earlier, Flaxville took the lead for the first time. They expanded the lead to four points, and we started to foul a little earlier than we needed to in that game, losing our poise a little bit. We just weren't used to trailing in the second half of games. The machine was breaking down, and the script of sweeping through the tournaments with championships at every stop was beginning to unravel. Flaxville was playing very deliberate on offense after they got the lead, but there was still a lot of time left. We hung within two points until late in the game, when Flaxville made their free throws (14–17 in the fourth quarter) and ended up winning the game 59–52, ending the dream of the perfect sweep, and violating the script.

No "I" in Team

Offensively, this game was probably the best individual game I had ever played, but still our team lost. I made 13–15 shots from the floor, many of them would have been three-pointers, and was 9–9

Rocky Nelson holds the first-place trophy up for Flaxville,
1979 Divisional championship. Plentywood Herald photo.

from the line. It was uncharacteristic for our team for that to happen, because we averaged four players in double figures. We just weren't ourselves that night, and we had lost our balance on offense. This was a phenomenon that had occurred previously in my high school career, and it would happen again on this night, of all nights. It is important to remember that what made the 1978 and 1979 Panthers so good was how well we played together as a team. It wasn't individual performances that won games, but a cohesive unit of five guys on the court and everyone on the team pulling together to do whatever we needed to do to win. Some players were role players, like Ray Chapman, who played great defense and rebounded and passed to the shooters; Joel Dighans was a tremendous rebounder and defender and he could score too. Bernie Wasser, a great passer and ball handler, could score when we needed him to. Jon and I would handle the ball and control the tempo of the game, and we were the scorers—that was our role. In 1978, Bill Fladager was a great passer and rebounder; Roger Trang was also a great passer and rebounder, and he could score a lot too. Both Roger and Bill were great defenders as well.

It is interesting to note that in the four highest-scoring games I had in my high school career (44, 42, 36 and 35 points), we lost three of those games, and it is no fun to score a lot of points and lose. In each of those games, I shot extremely well from the field. I didn't take bad shots and shoot us out of the game; it is just that when one scorer gets really hot like that, the rest of the team can tend to neglect their own need to contribute to the scoring effort, and the offense as a whole suffers as a result.

It is also important to note that although Robin Selvig of Outlook holds the three-game scoring average at State Class C tourney at 112 points, his 1970 team did not make it past the morning round, whereas the 1978 Outlook team of Dave Selvig, Randy Wangerin and Jerry West won the State championship, and typically they would each score about 15–18 points a game, or something like that. Their team was so good because of how brilliantly those three guys played together as a team. And that is why they won.

Now, I'm happy to report that the true Panthers would return to the court at the State tournament two weeks later, but the games against Opheim and Flaxville at Divisionals were rough games for us. I mentioned previously that we had peaked as a team at the District tournament championship game against Flaxville two weeks earlier, and that was indeed the case.

How Sad Can You Be?

It was a bitter, disappointing loss, but I remember thinking after the game, "You know what? We're going to the Big Dance again. How sad can you be?" We had not achieved our goal of the clean sweep, but we still had a chance to win the big one. That is one of the beautiful things about the basketball tournament system in Montana: it is very forgiving. You can make a mistake, *two* mistakes in fact, and *still* make it to State tournament, and even *win* it. Don't forget, Outlook didn't even win the District championship the year before after we upset them, and they went on to win State. Peerless had defeated Westby in 1975, also at District, and Westby went on to win State as well. If in both of those years District 1-C was only sending two teams to Divisional, neither Westby or Outlook would have even advanced to Divisional, and they never would have been crowned State champion. I also didn't know it at the time, but in 1979, we had also beaten the eventual State champion in the District championship game, Flaxville. That meant that in a span of five years, 1975–79, Peerless would beat the eventual State champion three times at District.

So what we needed to do was put this game behind us. And we did. I do remember looking up at our Pep Club after the game and they were disappointed too. They had a lot of confetti they were going to throw after we won. But there would be no nets, and no confetti. Some of our fans, not knowing what else to do with the confetti after the game, threw it up in the air anyway. That's what it's for, right?

But in the end, the Peerless Panthers we were moving onto State.

The Dark Lord of Basketball

I have a confession to make (since I am still Catholic). That day at the picture window, the day before the challenge game against Flaxville in 1978, when Dad and I stood there looking out, Dad really did sell his soul to the Dark Lord of Basketball. Well, actually it was mine he sold, if you remember the story. I always had my suspicions, but he came clean with me many years later, at the State tournament in Bozeman in 1995, right before the Pep Rally before the championship game. I just kept pressing him on the matter and he finally caved in and told me. Yep, Tiny was in cahoots with the Dark Lord of Basketball. I knew it! It turns out the Dark Lord of Basketball was a Fallen Angel from Flaxville. Now, this bit of information surprised me, not because the Dark Lord was from Flaxville—in fact I sort of expected that—but because it was so hard for me to imagine there was ever an angel from Flaxville.

So, after Dad came clean, I had a lot of questions, you know, like how did he do it? Who was involved? Stuff like that. I wanted to know the details. One thing I wanted to know was why did he have to make it so dramatic every game? Why couldn't it have been a blowout? I mean, if you're going to sell your soul to the Dark Lord, can't you get your money's worth and have a nice, relaxing blowout? Dad told me he held off for as long as he could in each game, before he sold out, to see how things would go first. Against Outlook in District semi-finals in 1978, he saw Outlook race to that eight-point lead early in the 2nd quarter and he panicked: He had a flashback to the Outlook gym three weeks earlier where they blew us off the court and we were behind 41–19 at half, so he couldn't wait any longer, before the game got out of hand. He sold his soul early in that one, right there early in the 2nd quarter. How did he do it? A little pitch-forked devil with horns (and a Flaxville jersey on; you think it's a coincidence the devil is red, hmm, do you now?) stood right there on Rollie Sullivan's left shoulder and told him to leave Dave Selvig in the game after he picked up his third foul in the second quarter. "Go on, go on, Rollie, it's ok; keep Dave in the game, he won't pick up his fourth foul." Do you think Rollie Sullivan would have done that in his right mind? He didn't do it at Divisionals a week later. Coincidence? I think not.

So what about the challenge game against Flaxville, where Dad would hock my soul, what happened there? In that game, Dad told me he waited until the fourth quarter, when we were behind by eight points. He held out as long as he could again, but then he had the Dark Lord knock Bernie Wasser unconscious and Bernie came out and scored eight points in the fourth quarter. I knew there had to be something sinister going on in that challenge game: How else do you think Bernie could have predicted we'd win by exactly nine points on the bus ride down? You see, it's all coming together now, isn't it?

So, to get us out of District in 1978, we lost Dad's soul; then, in the challenge game against Flaxville, it was mine; and now, after the Opheim game, it would be Jon's, which Dad had been holding in strategic reserve all this time, just in case we needed it to get to State in 1979. Once again, Dad held out as long as he could, waiting all the way into overtime this time! Man, that was close, Dad! So you can see that he was struggling with this; he didn't just willy-nilly hock our souls before the game started; he figured he'd wait and see how things went first, but he would take it to the bitter edge against

Opheim. In "the call that could have gone either way", as referee Myron Gackle flipped an imaginary coin in his head to see if he would blow his whistle or not—heads it's a charge; tails it's not—the Dark Lord made the coin come up heads. Myron shrilly blew his whistle, called the foul, and Jon made the free throws to send the Peerless Panthers to State. Phew! Now that was cutting it close!

So naturally, after Dad told me all this, I was a little concerned about his future in the afterlife, but thanks to the wonders of modern technology and instant text messaging, I have been reassured by my grandpa (who sent me a text message from heaven) that Dad is up there in heaven, where he ought to be. When I sent a short message, "Is Dad up there?" Grandpa sent back a simple, quick message: "Yep."

So how does that work? Three souls lost and somehow Dad gets them all back. Leave it up to Tiny. So this is the scoop Grandpa gave me about how Dad got back into heaven. Apparently Dad was making the Dark Lord of Basketball miserable in hell. Man, how do you do *that?* Yes, well, Dad was *so* miserable he couldn't play basketball down there that the Dark Lord himself couldn't stand it, so he finally just booted Dad out. The devil's reasoning was thus: Tiny couldn't play basketball in heaven either, so he'd be miserable up there too, which is the whole point of hell, so why don't I just send him up there and then I don't have to listen to him complain anymore, but he'll still be suffering. Grandpa told me the Dark Lord's last words to Dad were, "And take your two boys back too, whenever they get here, because I got a feeling they're a lot like their father!"

So I thought, "Fair enough. Great! At least Dad's in heaven, and Jon and I can rest easy too." But then I thought, "He's got to still be miserable up there because he can't play basketball, right?" Nope. This is where it gets good. Grandpa told me, "Tiny snuck a rim, a net, six balls, and an air pump past St. Peter, and he's up here playing basketball with the Pirates in heaven, right now."

"How did he do that? " I asked.

"Well," Grandpa said, "If Tiny figured out a way to play basketball in North Africa by sneaking a portable gym past the U.S. Army in World War II, don't you think he can get one past St. Peter? St. Peter is a very trusting fellow, you know. How else do you think he got the job? You think they hire cynical people in heaven?"

"But Grandpa," I replied. "The Dark Lord said there was no basketball in heaven."

Grandpa's response was, "That was before Tiny got here. You boys bring your sneakers with you when you come up here 'cause you're gonna play!"

"Awesome!" I said. "Hey grandpa, can we get a rematch against Flaxville for the State championship up there?"

"Nope. I'm afraid that can't be arranged," Grandpa replied.

"Why not?" I asked.

"Because there ain't nobody from Flaxville up here."

The Fallout

Sunday night at the Puckett home in Peerless, the day following the Divisional championship game against Flaxville, Jon basically had what had to be close to a nervous breakdown. He was crying uncontrollably, and Mom and Dad were trying to comfort him. I knew why he was upset, of course, because I had a lot of the same feelings. What was happening was the expectation that we had put on ourselves to run a clean sweep through the tournaments had become a burden on us. We also didn't want to disappoint the Peerless community, although that was a ridiculous thought because they always supported us, win or lose. But one thing that happened caught our attention. Because of the expectation that we were headed to State again, many people in Peerless decided not to reserve hotel rooms in Plentywood or Wolf Point. Now if we lost it wasn't only us, our team, that would be disappointed, but the Peerless community too, and we didn't want to disappoint our greatest supporters! Of course, that was a ridiculous thought, but nevertheless we didn't want to disappoint. We felt like we were carrying the flag for the entire community, and we really wanted to win not just for ourselves, but everyone in Peerless. After Divisionals, the tough part was over, but the fallout, the residue and aftershocks of that emotional game against Opheim were so intense that I think the reaction Jon had Sunday night was because he finally had time to let out what he was feeling, had been all through the day Saturday, but hadn't been able to express because we'd had to prepare for Flaxville that night.

But we could relax now and let it all out. We had made it back to State! But those two days in Wolf Point, Friday and Saturday, were very tough on all of us emotionally . . .

One Relieved Man

On Monday morning at school, the first day back to school following Divisionals, my first period was study hall, a free hour. This was the coolest hour of my life. I mean, to start the week at school after a weekend of basketball with a free period, which I had deliberately and calculatingly planned out that year, was awesome. I would read the Billings Gazette about all the weekend games, then I'd check out of study hall and go down to the gym and shoot around in my socks. I'd get a ball and walk slowly around the basket, shooting set shots, working on my shooting form and mechanics, and I'd relax and run the images of the previous weekend's games through my mind. It was pure bliss.

On this particular morning, Coach Niccum (also free during this time) sauntered into the gym to join me in my routine. Folks, let me tell you, this was one relieved man. As I wrote earlier, in the previous two years he had coached—at Opheim in 1977 and Scobey in 1978—his teams had *high* expectations to make it to State and do well, and both years he did not make it, losing tough games in the tournament to end the season. The way he had drilled us in practice all year, and the video we watched against Opheim on Saturday afternoon after the close game against them Friday night, were just two examples of how he was bound and determined not to let this happen again. Now he had finally, after two frustrating seasons with those teams, made it to the Big Dance with the Panthers. The pressure was off for him, and I was seeing him smile a lot more than I had previously. In fact, I think that Monday we might not have had practice, the first Monday all season that we would not have a practice.

So Niccum and I were talking about the Flaxville game on that hallowed Panther court on this fine Monday morning, and I was telling him how I was disappointed we didn't win the championship against Flaxville and he said, "Hey, we're there, man," indicating that we were headed to Helena, and that is all that mattered to him. Now, although we did not have practice that day, Coach Jim Niccum did not have the day off: Later that night, the strategic brain trust of the Panthers, Tiny Puckett and Jim Niccum, would meet again at another mystical late-night beer séance at the Puckett house for a critical session entitled, "How to Beat the Triangle and Two."

A Total Eclipse of the Sun

On this same, peculiar Monday, February 26, 1979, a total eclipse of the sun would occur over Northeastern Montana, with the heart of the darkness occurring straight above our heads in Peerless. Our science teacher, Pat Haas, had prepared us to look at the eclipse through these pinholes in shoe boxes, or something like that, but I didn't use it. I just wanted to walk around outside and experience the sensation of being engulfed in almost total darkness in the daytime in Peerless. It is very unusual to experience a total solar eclipse where you live; at any point on the earth's surface, this phenomena occurs only once almost every 400 years, and it just so happened that this total solar eclipse over Peerless occurred the Monday following the Divisional tournament in Wolf Point. As you have probably gleaned by now, everything I experienced that year was placed into the context of our team's ride to State. *Everything.* So my mind was focused exclusively on basketball, and this is why I remember that solar eclipse: I saw it as a metaphor for the shadow that had been cast over our team after the shocking close call we'd had with Opheim on Friday night, and the loss to Flaxville in the Divisional championship game just two days earlier. The dream of a clean sweep through the tournaments was now gone, *eclipsed;* and worse, there were now doubts about going forward and winning the

State championship. I saw the shadow of the total solar eclipse of the sun over Peerless that day as a smudge on our perfection, and the only thing I could think of on that bizarre Monday, as the entire population of Peerless scuttled around the streets in almost total darkness, was that, strangely, approximately 32 miles to the east, the sun was somehow shining brilliantly over the town of Flaxville.

The Second Beer Séance

The next weird thing that happened that Monday was the beer séance at the Puckett house later that night. Now, the first thing you do prior to conducting a beer séance is analyze the threat. What defense were we going to see against Custer our first game at State? Jon and I had already pulsed our informant in Scobey, Kelly Norman, on this matter, but he didn't have anything for us. He didn't have any contacts in Custer (his sources were based primarily in Flaxville), so he couldn't really help us, just wished us well. But it turned out we didn't even need Kelly on this one, because the probability of us facing a triangle and two against Custer at State was so overwhelmingly likely, that Jon and I didn't pursue any other leads, although Dad would check with his sources on the Pony Express rural mail route in Opheim. The reason we thought we were going to see the triangle and two against Custer was simple. Think about it. Opheim had virtually stymied our offense with it at Divisional, holding us to our lowest point total of the year against a class C team, and one of the lowest point totals ever in high school. And Opheim's assistance coach, Steve Keller, was the older brother of Custer's star player, Jeff Keller, so we had a hunch Opheim might share their film on us with Custer, and they did. Dad did collect this much intel from his contacts in Opheim, and that was the only info he and Jim Niccum would need to know. It was predicted that when we ran out onto the court in Helena less than two weeks later to face Custer, we were going to see a triangle and two. The threat was analyzed.

Well, Coach Niccum and Dad had picked the perfect "day" to hold the mystical beer séance to summon the basketball spirits and ask them to channel how to beat the triangle and two defense. But just so you know, there were no more dealings with the Dark Lord of Basketball, now that Dad had gotten us to State again with referee Myron Gackle's coin flip charging call against Norm Dyrland and Opheim on Friday night. These were celestial, playful basketball spirits he was dealing with now. They knew how to beat this defense, and they had been stirred into action by witnessing the devastating effects this defense had on Peerless Friday night against Opheim. And then they were prepped for action, if you will, by the strange occurrence of the total eclipse of the sun over Peerless earlier that day. And the beauty was they wanted *nothing* in return. The only thing required to summon them was an absolute passion, a pure *love* for the game of basketball, and an unyielding desire to know the truth about anything related to the game, in this case, how to beat the triangle and two defense. So when Coach Niccum and Dad summoned them to our kitchen table in the Puckett house that night, after a few preparatory beers of their own, it didn't take much coaxing for the spirits to arrive . . .

As I sat in the living room listening to the bizarre ritual, as I had done during many beer séances at our house that winter, I started to think on my own, before the spirits came, about what the solution would be to beat this defense. At that point, I knew two solutions that wouldn't work: 1) We had tried our passing game offense; that didn't work because three people were playing a zone in that defense, so they just stood there and watched us run around and set screens; and 2) We had tried to run our zone offense and that didn't work either; two of their people shadowed our best shooters wherever we cut on the floor, so there were no gaps to attack. So it had to be something different than our passing game and zone offense. But what could it be?

When the spirits arrived, I strained my ears to hear the answer, and the soft answer came back, *"Set screens . . . "* And I thought, oh great, that's the best you can do? We already do that in our passing game offense, pass and screen away, pass and screen away, come off screens, receive a pass, and shoot. This offense explains why of the 30 field goals we averaged in a game in 1979, 21 of them came off an assist, a pass off a screen. But we already tried that against Opheim and it didn't work, so what's up? Oh, wait. That wasn't all. There's more. I strained my ears to hear the sweet, soft voice of the benevolent basketball spirit speaking to Coach Niccum and my dad from the other side of the basketball world, and this is what I heard: *"Set screens on the ball . . ."*

Oh my God, it was so simple! Back to the basics, back to when we were kids in the old gym, the old screen and roll. Basketball 101. Why would it work? For two reasons: 1) Because of all the one on one Jon and I played, we both shot better off the dribble anyway. So when we received the screen from either Bernie or Ray on the free throw line extended, the plan was for us to pop that jump shot right then and there off the dribble. We couldn't continue to dribble to drive to the basket because we'd run right into the zone if we did that. But what about the defender on Bernie and Ray switching out onto Jon and me after the screen was set? This is the second reason it would work: 2) Since the defenders on Ray and Bernie were plopped down on the blocks in the triangle zone, there wouldn't be any defender to switch out on us! That meant that if Bernie and Ray set a good screen, Jon and I would get a good look off the dribble (me to the left and Jon to the right) and get the jump shot off. The only way it wouldn't work would be if the defender fought through the screen. Joel Dighans would float in the middle of the triangle, keeping them all at home in the paint, so that solved the problem of anyone coming out of the triangle to stop the shot. If any of those guys left the triangle we would pop it into Joel and he would shoot his deadly jump shot right in the paint. The séance closed with a simple "Thank You" from Coach Niccum and my dad, with another cold one raised to christen the decision.

Practice Makes Perfect

So in practice the next day, we began to tryout our new complex, multi-faceted offense against Custer: The simple screen and roll. Joe left and Jon right. Bernie and Ray were taught not to roll to the basket, but just pop out after the screen, either for a wide open 10–

15 footer, or as a release point to start the next sequence of the screen on the other side of the court.

So, did it work? We will have to wait and see how this offense worked against Custer at State, but I'll give you a little hint: We lit it up against Custer in the first half at State with our most explosive scoring output in one half. But I'll have to provide the gory details of the Battle of the Helena PE Center against Custer a little later.

And all of this from those gentle, benevolent, sweet little basketball spirits, so willing to assist you if you just ask sincerely, from the heart, with a couple beers, on a day when a rare total eclipse of the sun has just passed over your head . . .

The Greatest Fans Ever

Once again, the community support for us in 1979 was overwhelming. Two hundred and thirty five tickets to the 1979 State tournament were sold out of Peerless High School that year. That is an amazing number of tickets, considering our enrollment was only 39 kids that year. An article in the Daniels County Leader identified only some of the people who purchased those 235 tickets, as another Peerless High School reunion was forming in Helena, Montana: Gussie and Virginia Whipple of Washington, Bob and Idella Singer of Ft. Benton, former Superintendent Marvin and Tedi Hash of Oregon; Bill Puckett of Idaho; Willis and Marie Haagenson of Highwood; Bruce and Ben Haagenson of Billings; from Park City, former Peerless coach of the late 30's Basil Helegeson and his wife Viola; Ole Peterson of Vancouver, Washington; from Billings, Jim and Anita Humphrey and their daughter; Leona Rigler of Livingston and her daughter Paula of Bozeman; John and Marsha Neill, Father Nyquist and Poppa Ray, all of Geraldine; Maurice Ackerman and wife and Eldon Ackerman and wife of Belgrade; Ronnie Trangsrud of Idaho; Gerry Girard of Harlem; Kenny Richardson of Bozeman; Kent and Lois Bray of Bozeman; Rollin Rieger, former coach and teacher, of Broadview; Butch and Pixine Zieske of Joliet; and Tim and Patsy Guenther of Park City.

Coming from Billings were Dave and Ronnie Sherman; Dennie

and Bonnie Ferestad and children; Kathleen and Willard Fladager; Wally and Margie Fladager; Ed Puckett and Ben Lien from Peerless, but spending the winters in Arizona they came for the tournament. Former coach Clark Shaffer, who took us to State the previous year, and wife Donna from Charlo. Alan and Lyle Knudson came from Wolf Point; Arden Nelson and wife of Williston; Anton and Shirley Dighans of Bozeman; Elaine Bersagel's parents came from Malta and Judy Alley's parents came from Joplin; Richard and Veanne Hawbaker from Shelby; Dianne Puckett Beesley and daughter Sara of Denver; Jim Bailey of Kalispell; Perry Thieven of Laramie, Wyoming and his uncle and aunt, the Bud Willards of Columbia Falls. Former teacher and coach, Larry Kolste and wife Shiela came from Fairfield; and Terry Michel.

Some Peerless people from Helena were Doris Lystad Drake and son; Greg Jackson; Maureen Dighans; Melissa and Joe Anderson; Representative Art Lund and his wife Cleo; Laura Kasseth King and son Matt.

Just to name a few . . . As always, the support from our community was overwhelming.

The Return
of the Panther

The Journey to Helena

Super Panther,
Annabelle Fouhy, 1979.

After another rousing, extremely creative Pep Rally on Monday night, organized by our fabulous cheerleaders (once again Super Panther stole the show! Who is that masked Panther?!!!), we left for State again on Tuesday morning. As we snaked our way across and down the beautiful state of Montana, I wanted the bus ride down to Helena to last forever. I can remember Niccum having us run line drills in Northern Montana College's gym along the way, but I think we got to run the "Blitz Drill," our favorite, so it wasn't all bad. Besides, these would be the last line drills I would have to run that season! However, I also knew this would be my last bus ride for basketball in high school, so I had mixed emotions as we headed to State: I was *so* excited about playing at State again, of course, but this was also going to be my last weekend of high school basketball, and I did not relish that thought. Not at all.

When the bus crested the hill one more time in 1979, and I

looked down into the Helena Valley, I felt like I was coming home. All of the memories of the magical experience we had the year before, when the people of Helena adopted us as their favorite sons, came flooding back to me, and it was a great feeling to know we had accomplished what we had set out to do: Return to Helena, even if we had lost the Divisional championship to Flaxville. But that didn't matter to me at all anymore. We were at the Big Dance again! I remember the letter we had received from Howard Retz in Helena the year before that congratulated us on our tournament run and ended with, "All Helena is looking forward to your return." So we were coming back to Helena, the state capitol, and also, at the time, the state capitol of Class C basketball, as this would be the 23rd consecutive year that Helena would host the State Class C basketball tournament.

It was remarkable what a different experience it would be for us as we entered Helena in 1979 than what it was in 1978. This time, *everyone* in Helena and at the State C tournament knew who Peerless was. The year before, *nobody* knew, except for Outlook and their fans, because we had beaten them twice. I stated earlier that if given the choice between being the underdog or the favorite, I'd pick the underdog, but that was on the court. Off the court, at the annual banquet on Wednesday night welcoming the teams to Helena, and hosted by the Helena Chamber of Commerce at the Colonial Inn, it felt good, *really* good, to know that as each coach stood up and introduced his team, it was our team that needed little introduction. And reading the Helena Independent Record earlier that day, a coach's poll taken prior to the tournament had picked Flaxville, followed by Peerless, as the pre-tourney favorites to win it all. The year before, we weren't expected to win a game. Also, can you believe Peerless was *not* the smallest school in the tournament that year? Willow Creek carried that distinction, with an enrollment of 32 kids.

Tiny and Faustine Puckett at State tournament, 1979.
Helena Independent Record photo by Bill Bowman.

Two Most Valuables

Two previous State tourney MVPs, Jon Puckett and Kevin Hatfield. Helena Independent Record photo by Bill Bowman.

One very unusual thing at the 1979 State tournament was that two previous State Class C tournament MVPs, Kevin Hatfield from Flaxville (1976) and Jon Puckett from Peerless (1978), were playing in the tournament. That had never happened before, and to my knowledge, it hasn't happened since. So at the banquet, Bill Bowman from the Helena Independent Record grabbed Jon and Kevin and had them pose for the camera, as if they were having a casual conversation in the Colonial following the banquet. I remember looking at Jon and Kevin thinking, "Wow, are they actually going to stand next to each other like that?" Well, I guess for the camera, anything.

A Cardinal Sin (Almost)

In the first afternoon game of the State tournament, Flaxville played St. Regis and played absolutely horridly. I remember watching the game thinking, "Oh, come on, St. Regis, get them out of the way, get them out of here," because I knew how much trouble we would have if we had to play Flaxville again. They had figured out our press, and defensively they were shutting us down as a team. I just wanted them out of the winner's bracket, and St. Regis came close, oh so close, to upsetting them that afternoon. Flaxville came out in the third quarter and scored two points—count them two—in the entire quarter, and looked like a junior high team on offense. I couldn't believe this was the same team we had played at Divisional just two weeks earlier. I'm thinking, "Okay, this is Flaxville's bad game. This is the time they could get nipped just like us against Opheim. So come on, baby." St. Regis led by seven points with four minutes left in the fourth quarter, but Flaxville started playing a little better and somehow managed to crawl back into it and tied the game at the end of regulation.

So Flaxville had survived regulation (just like we had against Opheim) and ended up winning the game 66–61 in overtime. I knew right when that buzzer sounded to end the game that Flaxville had dodged a bullet, and that they had gotten their bad game out of their system. Flaxville always had the potential to play absolutely horribly offensively, but their defense was always consistently good, and that is why they won. I always thought, "Why can't they play that way against us?" After their win against St. Regis, I had the sinking feeling they would breeze through their semi-final game (which would be against Roberts) and we would have to play them again for the championship. The thing is, teams that hadn't played us before couldn't handle our pressure, both on offense and on defense, because they had never seen anything like our team's quickness before. But Flaxville had seen it four times, and had learned how to deal with it.

Six-Foot-and-Under

So the last game of the day was Peerless vs. Custer, and everyone at State was buzzing about it. Because this basically was a six-foot-and-under matchup at the State tournament, it was a dream game for the Helena fans. Both teams had wide-open styles, and the Helena fans, as well as everyone else at the State tournament, were really looking forward to the game. It was a lot like when the fans had enjoyed watching us play against Outlook in northeastern Montana the year before.

I got the assignment to guard Jeff Keller, who averaged 26

points a game and had scored over 50 twice that season. We were playing Custer straight man-to-man, as we always did, and I was very focused on shutting Keller down. But in the first two minutes of the game, I got two quick fouls called on me, as the ref was calling the game ridiculously close. I got called for hand checks on him, which no one had called on me up in northeast Montana all year. So that I wouldn't pick up my third foul, I had to switch off of him after that. In the meantime, Jon went down with some kind of injury; so, early on, I was playing with two fouls and Jon was out of the game. Not a great start to State for the Panthers. Later in the half, I picked up my third foul, but Niccum left me in (very risky, but it worked) because Jon was on the bench at that time too.

Offensively, we came out sizzling, and the offense Niccum had drawn up against the triangle and two was working beautifully. The screens Bernie and Ray were setting were freeing Jon and me up for shots, and we weren't missing. We led 21–17 after the first quarter; then, in the second quarter, we broke the game open, running our fast break and getting shots off that triangle and two. Just absolutely lit it up against them. It was fantastic. It was like a run-and-gun shootout six-foot-and-under tournament, and we were just dazzling the crowd with our passing and fast break, and our offense against the triangle and two. It was pure *joy* to be able to do that on that stage. Not even the year before, when we were the run-and-gun Panthers, had we had such an explosive half in a tournament, so after what had happened at Divisional this was just an incredible experience. Our team was so much more relaxed in its play than it had been at Divisionals against Opheim and Flaxville. The pressure was off now, and we were back to ourselves. We would come very close in this game to placing not four, but five Panthers in double figures.

We scored 48 points at halftime and led 48–31. We had systematically demolished the triangle and two with Bernie and Ray setting screens on the ball for Jon and me. Against Opheim, we had scored only 49 points in the *entire* game, and now here we had 48 points at *halftime* against Custer. It was the biggest scoring half we'd had the entire season. We had scorched the nets on 20–30 shooting as a team; I was 7–10. The problem was at halftime we had some foul trouble, and this would catch up with us later in the game.

Cruise Control

In the second half, because we had such a large lead, I deliberately held back from shooting to ensure the rest of the team got involved in the game offensively. I didn't want to let what had happened at Divisional against Flaxville happen again at State. Because we had such a large lead, this was the perfect opportunity to pull back. I had a lot of opportunities for shots, and I passed them up to make sure we had that balance. I took only three shots the entire second half, probably the lowest number of shots I had taken in a half since I was a freshman, and this was at State.

Late in the second quarter, Custer had switched out of the triangle and two and gone straight man-to-man. It was a much better defense for them. We kind of put it in cruise control in the third quarter and just played them even. Then, with about six minutes left in the game, we pushed the lead up to 20 points, 66–46, and I said to myself "This game's over, this is a blowout." After that, our foul trouble caught up to us (Dighans fouled out, I had four) and Custer mounted a furious comeback, but I knew the game was out of reach and was never bothered at all when they cut the lead to seven points with less than a minute left in the game. I knew we were moving on to play Willow Creek the next night in the semi-finals.

The headline in the following day's Independent Record made me smile: "Balanced attack lifts Peerless past Custer." The Panthers were back. Jon led us with 23 points, Joe 16, Joel 15, Ray 10 and Bernie 8. Almost five players in double figures. Great balance, and a great start to State.

Defensive Lapse

Now, there was somebody on our bench who was a little bit more than bothered about Custer's comeback. Remember when I wrote about Niccum coaching Opheim in 1977 District 3-C Tourney against Hinsdale in the morning game? Opheim was leading by eight points with 52 seconds left, and then lost the game. I think Niccum had a horrible flashback to that game at the end of the Custer game. He was terrified that we were going to blow a 20-point lead in the fourth quarter. I really didn't understand what all the fuss was about, but he was livid with our defense and ripped into Bernie Wasser after the game. It was awful. Bernie was crying, I remember that. Jon and I were both in foul trouble so we couldn't guard Keller, and Custer was setting double and triple screens for Keller and he started to really score some points. But Custer had a really good team; they were capable of scoring like we could, and they had played very well in the second half. Now that I look back on it, I see why Niccum was upset with our defense: The 67 points we gave up against Custer was the largest number of points we had allowed the entire season. Not even Scobey had scored that many points against us. So we have our best half offensively in the first half and our worst half defensively in the second half. Funny game. Final score was 74–67.

So the Panthers moved on to play Willow Creek in the semi-finals. One more win and we'd be in the Big One, the State championship. One more win . . .

Defense Wins

We played Willow Creek Friday night in the second semi-final game. They had a very good team; they were the Western Division Champions and had lost only one game to a class C team all year, and had only two losses overall. They were well coached, and one of the things that concerned me about them was the coach's son, Mark Korich; he played point guard, and I thought he might be able to handle our defensive pressure, which would take away one of our most lethal weapons.

This would be a strange game for me offensively. I consider this the best game I ever played, even though I would go 0–5 from the floor in the first half. Prior to Willow Creek, in the last five games of the tournament, spanning Flaxville at District championship and through the game against Custer the night before, I had shot 52–72 from the floor. Then at State against Willow Creek I came out and went 0–5. The reason I consider it my best game is because I stayed in my game, trusted my teammates to pick up the slack offensively, played very well defensively against their point guard Mark Korich, and passed off for a lot of assists to the rest of the team. I could have forced the game and become frustrated; instead I "let the game come to me," as Dad always said, and it worked.

Actually, our entire team played brilliantly on defense that night, and that is why we won. Jon was guarding their leading scorer, Dana Williams, a forward (remember Jon would guard the other team's forward because Bernie defended the two guard); he held him to 15 points and he averaged over 20. We also had a balanced attack offensively, almost placing four players in double figures again, which is what we averaged.

Prior to the game, I remember watching Flaxville play Roberts in the first half. They had gotten that miserable game out of their system the night before and looked good. In the second half, they pulled away from Roberts and I remember that while we were sitting in the locker room waiting to come out onto the court to play Willow Creek a loud ROAR came from the entire crowd. Couldn't figure out what it was, but we later learned that David Weltikol, one of Flaxville's forwards, had scored on a breakaway slam dunk and the entire Helena crowd had gone nuts. He was only about 6'1", but could high jump 6'9".

After the explosive 48-point first half we had against Custer the night before, and Niccum's explosion at us for our defensive lapse in the second half, we came out against Willow Creek, very much focused on the defensive end of the court. Both teams were playing good defense, and at the end of the first quarter Willow Creek led 13–12. They were a good team, and I knew it was going to be a tough game, but because we were playing so well as a team again offensively, I felt really good about the way ahead in that game. One key thing was that two of their starters were in foul trouble; Rick Lamb and Dana Williams both had three fouls at the end of the first quarter. Although we hadn't scored many points, our quickness so outmatched them that they couldn't keep up with us defensively and were forced to foul us in order to defend.

In the second quarter we executed our half court offense flaw-lessly, scoring 18 points in the quarter to take a 30–24 lead at halftime. The five of us were passing and screening, moving around like a machine; passes to Dighans underneath for layups, Bernie shooting well; it just felt so good to be executing again after those two horrible games we had against Opheim and Flaxville at Divi-sional. And all of this without me scoring a single point in the first half.

Pressure and Denial

At halftime Niccum knew he had to do something to get me into the game offensively, so he called a couple plays to start the second half wherein I would come off a double screen on the baseline to get freed up for a good look, get a shot to go down, and then maybe get into a groove. That happened at the beginning of the second half; I got a good screen, got a good look, and got my first shot to go down. After that, I shot 6–10 from the floor in the second half. Now, with me back in the game offensively, our offense really started to click, and we continued to execute in the half court like we had never done before. We were playing brilliantly offensively.

But it was our defense in that quarter that won the game for us. Willow Creek ran an offense with a single point guard; they didn't go with a two-guard front. Mark Korich ran the point, and I started to really pressure him full court. When he crossed half court, I kept the pressure on and forced him to pick up his dribble several times. In the meantime, Jon, Bernie and Ray were denying the entry pass into the wings, so several times down the court Willow Creek couldn't get into their offense. I mean, not even get a shot off. Then, when the wings were able to get the ball, they were pushed so far away from the basket they were out of their range and couldn't get a good shot off. We basically shut them down completely, and this number-one seed from the West, which had a great scoring offense, would only manage four points against us that quarter. We outscored them 14–4 in the quarter, and took a 44–28 lead into the fourth quarter.

Joe Puckett drives against Willow Creek, State C semi-final, 1979.
Helena Independent Record photo by Bill Bowman.

Balancing Act

Coming out to start the fourth quarter, we were eight minutes away from the State championship game. Eight minutes away from reaching the goal we had set for ourselves before the season began. We were close. We continued to pressure them relentlessly on defense, and, with about four minutes left, we pushed the lead to 52–34; the game, although it was moving slowly, was now getting close to a blowout. We kept forcing them out and away from the basket on defense. I thought we might even hold them to under 40 points in the game. But just like Custer did the night before, Willow Creek mounted a comeback of their own, cutting the lead to ten points with about two minutes left. They pressed us, of all things, and did force a couple turnovers and converted them to baskets. But Niccum called a timeout and we regrouped, came back out and broke the press and started to pull away again, eventually winning the low-scoring contest 57–46. As the final seconds counted down, our cheerleaders started the "Power's in the East, Power's in the East" chant, and then, on the opposite side of the court, Flaxville joined in. Strange how the two rivals could do that. But less than 24 hours later the two towns would not be cheering in unison.

The next morning, the Independent Record quoted Niccum as saying, "The big thing about this ballclub is its team concept of the game. They all play together so well." Never before had Jon (17), Joe (15), Ray (3) , Bernie (8) and Joel (14) played so well together as a team, and we were now just one game away from winning it all. Why did it have to be Flaxville?

Focused

Saturday morning, the day of the State championship game, I chose not to attend the morning games at State. I wanted to stay focused in my room, relaxing and getting mentally prepared for the game that night, no distractions. This was the only time at a tournament I did not attend the morning session, but that was probably exactly what I needed to do. It is so enjoyable watching Class C basketball, and I enjoyed watching other games even while I was still playing in high school. But this was how seriously focused on winning it all I was, and I think the focus at that point might have been working against me, and perhaps the same was true for some of my teammates as well. Just *playing* in a Montana State C tournament is a once-in-a-lifetime experience (actually, for me, twice-in-a-lifetime, but I was lucky), and savoring every moment, including watching the exciting morning games, would probably have been a better decision.

The Dream Warm up

Running out onto the court to warm up for the State championship game was an absolutely unbelievable experience. I had shivers running up and down my spine. I looked up into the crowd and thought about all the times I had been sitting in those same stands, and watching this game as a spectator, going all the way back to 1975 when Westby won it. But now I was in this game myself, playing for the State Class C basketball championship in Montana. This was it. There was no game after this. There was no tomorrow. The dream of the State C basketball championship was now a real possibility.

With just minutes left before the State championship game started, the Peerless and Flaxville cheerleaders led the two towns in the "Power's in the East" chant again, and "Daniels County Final" as well. Both towns chanted in unison again. The Flaxville and Peerless cheerleaders also jointly unveiled the "Daniels County District 1-C" banner around the court before the game began, as they had done previously in Plentywood and Wolf Point. But after the teams were introduced, and both teams ran out onto the court for the opening tip, the old rivals heard the familiar "Go Panthers Go!" and "Go Cards Go!" chants ringing through the Carroll College PE Center, louder than they had ever been before, one final time in 1979.

There Can Be Only One

The game started at a faster pace than most Peerless-Flaxville games. Jon came out sizzling, lighting it up with jump shots off the dribble from both sides of the court. Jon again would have a spectacular State tournament, stepping up big as he always did in the big games. He came very close to winning the MVP for a second consecutive year.

But another player who came out hot in that game was not from Peerless: It was Kevin Hatfield from Flaxville. I had never seen him come out of the gate shooting like he was, and he wasn't missing. It was like he was possessed, playing *very* aggressively, both on offense and on defense, rebounding, blocking shots; he was playing at his absolute best in this big game, just like Jon always did in these big games. These were two former State tourney MVP's, Jon Puckett and Kevin Hatfield, playing like the MVPs they were, brilliantly, stepping up big in the big game. Joel Dighans had contained Hatfield very well the previous two games. In the championship game at Divisionals, Joel Dighans had held him to nine points. Then, earlier at the District championship game, Dighans had held him to 12 points. But not this game. I remember thinking to myself, "Where has this guy been all year?" Well, unfortunately for the Panthers, Kevin Hatfield had picked a great night to show up for the Cardinals. Actually, all of the Cardinals showed up that night. It was not the same team that played St. Regis two nights earlier, not even the same team we had played at Divisionals, and *definitely* not the team we had played at District tournament. Flaxville had yet to reach its ceiling.

On Another Level

But we were playing exceptionally well too. As good as Flaxville was playing, we were playing even better. Jon scored eight points in the first quarter, most of them on long-range jumpers, and we led 14–12 at the end of the quarter. In the second quarter, the lead changed hands a few times, and the game was tied four times in the quarter,

Jon Puckett uses a screen from Ray Chapman and drives against Rocky Nelson of Flaxville, first half of the state championship, 1979. Helena Independent Record photo by Bill Bowman.

Joe Puckett uses a screen from Bernie Wasser and drives against Russell Edwards and David Weltikol, first half of state championship, 1979. Helena Independent Record photo by Bill Bowman.

just as it had been in the first quarter. But as this game progressed, one of the things I started to notice about Flaxville's defense was that they were not playing me straight man-to-man anymore, like they had done at District and Divisional championship games, where I had scored 28 and 35 points against them. Also, earlier in the season at Peerless, I had scored 33 points against them. These would be three of the highest-scoring games I'd had that entire season, and Bakken was not about to let it happen again. This time, when I came off a screen away from the ball, or when Bernie or Ray set a screen for me on the ball, there was a quick switch out, and it was hard for me to get good looks at the basket. They were playing very sticky defense (as they always did), but I think Terry Bakken had told his team to not let me break loose against them again. And I didn't; I would score only 14 points in this game, with only four field goals, one of my lowest field goal outputs of that entire season, if not the lowest.

But we were playing sticky defense too. Jon's shooting was brilliant, and at the end of the first half we'd shut them down defensively and taken a 28–25 lead into the locker room. It felt good to have that lead going into the locker room. At that point, as good as we were playing, I felt great about our chances to win that game. But one troubling thing was the difficulty we were having forcing any turnovers off our pressure defense; we were not able to fast break against them. We needed to force the tempo to beat Flaxville; it was dangerous to play this team in a half court game, and this was a half court game. In the three wins we had against Flaxville that year, we would have short, quick-scoring bursts fueled by turnovers off the press and then fast-break baskets. We would go on 8–0 or 10–0 runs and break the game open, then play them evenly the rest of the game, shooting free throws in the end, and winning. But at the Divisional championship game, and then again at State, that run would never come. Their guards had figured out how to handle our pressure, and so we were forced to play that half court game against them. Once again, this would prove to be our demise against the Cardinals.

The Run that Didn't Come

We came out in the second half 16 minutes away from our goal of a State championship. Hatfield made a basket to start the second half, picking right up where he'd left off in the first half. Then Ray Chapman converted a three-point play, and Hatfield scored again to make it 31–29 Peerless. Chapman hit again, and then I scored on a fast-break layup following a Flaxville turnover (oh, is that run coming now?!!!). We led 35–29 with about four and half minutes left in the third quarter! This was the time for that run to come; this was the moment of the game, after that turnover and fast break-basket, for that run to come. We had pushed the lead to six points and now had a chance to break it open, as we always had to do against this team. Would that run come? Why wouldn't it come? What could we have done differently?

After I made the driving layup off a steal to make the score 35–29, I remember sprinting back down the court on defense thinking this was going to be it, this was going to be the run that would break their back again. But it didn't happen. In fact, the exact opposite happened. In the next three minutes of the third quarter, Flaxville went on an 11–0 run to take a 40–35 lead. With 4:33 left in the third quarter, Russell Edwards passed the ball inside to David Weltikol and Weltikol was fouled shooting. He made one of the two free throws and this started the run with which Flaxville would go on to end the third quarter. They scored the next 11 points of the game to take a 40–35 lead. I hit a shot at the top of the key, but then Flaxville closed the quarter out with another 4–0 run to take the lead 44–37 going into the fourth quarter. Their run to end the third quarter was 15–2. We had never had a run popped on us like that before. We were shaken up. This was so unusual because it was always Peerless that would come from behind and put a run like that on a team, scoring a flurry of points in a hurry. We weren't turning the ball over and we weren't taking bad shots; our shots were simply not falling, and we were only getting one shot. And Flaxville, on the other end, was not missing. In the third quarter, Jon and Joel were completely shutout from scoring, and Ray led the team with five

Jon Puckett defends Russell Edwards of Flaxville with 4:33 left in the third quarter and Peerless leading 35-29, as the scoreboard shows. Helena Independent Record photo by Bill Bowman.

Flaxville's David Weltikol scores first basket of fourth quarter
over Jon Puckett, extending Flaxville's devasting run.
Helena Independent Record photo by Bill Bowman.

points in the quarter. Also, Jon had picked up his third foul in the third quarter. He had to be careful because he was guarding Weltikol inside. Things were definitely not looking good to start the fourth quarter, to say the least.

And Then It Fell Apart

In the first few minutes of fourth quarter, Flaxville picked up right where they'd left off. They scored the first 8 of 10 points in the quarter, and stretched the lead to 52–39, completing a 23–4 run after we'd had the lead 35–29. Our shots continued falling short, and Flaxville started to break our press for easy baskets. The court seemed big, gigantic, like we couldn't cover everyone on it. I'm not sure if it is or not, but it seemed like the Carroll College PE Center court is actually bigger than Wolf Point's or Plentywood's court, where we played the Divisional and District tournaments. I remember thinking the same thing the previous year against Manhattan Christian in the semi-final game; they broke our press very well and scored a lot of easy baskets. Presses are more effective on smaller courts; there are fewer angles to cover on defense in order to intercept a pass, and there is simply less space to cover on defense when forcing a turnover.

I have often joked about going back in time to call a timeout and go into a four corners when we had the lead 35–29. Outlook would always do that when they got the lead against Flaxville, and they would be successful with it. But Dad would always say, "You've got to dance with the girl that brought you to the dance," meaning that we had to go with what got us into that championship game in the first place: Our full court pressure man-to-man defense and our attacking-passing game offense. And this is what we did. In the end, the full court pressure defense was picked apart by Flaxville's guards, and our passing game offense resulted in shots falling short. But hindsight is always 20/20. We gave it our best shot with our greatest strength—our quickness—but just came up a little short in the end. That same defensive quickness had shutdown Willow Creek the night before, holding them to a mere four points in the third quarter, but Flaxville had seen us too many times, had practiced against it, prepared for it, and, in the end, mastered it.

With about three minutes left, Flaxville led 56–41. The 1979 Panthers made their final push. Jon scored a three-point play and then I made two free throws. Then, after Hatfield made two free throws, Jon made another basket, cutting the lead to 58–47. At that point, we were still in it, pressing with a lot of energy and never giving up. But then Rocky Nelson made four straight points to put the game out of reach. I remember, when Rocky Nelson made the second of those two baskets, Bernie Wasser ,with both hands up in the air, literally threw himself at Rocky. I swear I saw the ball fly *through* Bernie's arms and into the basket. Rocky had never shot like that before. I so clearly remember Bernie's desperate lunge at Rocky as he tried to stop that shot. But it was just not to be. This was Flaxville's night to play the way they were capable of playing, to play in a way they had never before played against us. They literally peaked in the State championship game, which is a nice game to peak in, don't you think?

The Dream Becomes a Nightmare

The game was over after Nelson made those baskets, but still we continued to fight. It was kind of like as long as I kept running, pressing, defending, being active on the court, I wouldn't have time to think about what the situation was, that the outcome was certain. I didn't accept the reality that the game was out of reach, however, until there was a timeout called with less than a minute left to take the Flaxville's starters out. Peerless' dream of winning the State championship was now over. I completely broke down emotionally. Niccum sent us (the starters) back out onto the court, which I wish he hadn't done because in that final minute of my high school basketball career, I was actually crying on the court. It was the saddest thing to be playing against Flaxville's subs (who Bakken had setup in a 2–3 zone) at the end of the State championship game. Absolutely a nightmare.

It was sad that it had to end like this, but when I think about my

Dejected Panthers on the bench just moments after receiving
second place trophy at State, 1979.

experiences of playing basketball in Peerless, growing up with Jon
and my dad and my friends, this is not the game or the moment I
think about. But my emotions at that point were off the charts. This
was not just about losing the State championship game to Flaxville.
This was my last game in a Panther uniform. This was my last game
playing with Jon. This was the last time Dad would see his boys play
together in high school. This was the end of an era for me, an end to
the only life I'd known growing up to that point, and, in a matter of
seconds, it all came crashing down on me like a giant wave.

I could not keep myself together on the bench. Jon was always
better than me at controlling his emotions. I sometimes think maybe
I got more of my mother's Italian genes, but then I wonder how that
could be because we're identical twins! I remember after we received
the second-place trophy, Dad came down on the court to take some
last pictures of us in uniform. We were sitting on the bench after
receiving the trophy, and it was probably about that time that
Flaxville was receiving their first-place trophy. Dad kneeled down on

one knee. He looked down at the floor in front of us, his right index finger curled over the top part of his upper lip and his thumb on his chin, which is what he would do whenever he was deep in thought, usually sad. I remember looking at him from the bench where I was crying, and I saw the look of pain in his eyes as they looked back at me. All of you with children know there is absolutely nothing more painful than seeing your child hurt, knowing there is absolutely nothing you can do to console them, take away the pain. The pictures he took capture the deep disappointment of a group of boys who put everything they possibly could into accomplishing a goal, but still came up a little short in the end.

Left It on the Court

But when I look back on it, I feel proud of what we accomplished. Sitting there on that bench that night, looking out on to the court at Carroll College PE Center, I knew our team had put its entire heart and soul out there, and we had left it all out there. We had exhausted every last drop of our energy, emotionally, physically, and on every level, and that, in the end, is the measure of a winner, of a true champion. I said as much to the 1995 Panthers at the pep rally before their State championship game against Belt, I said if they gave it their best shot and left it all on the court, they too, would be champions. And that group of boys left everything out on the court as well. In fact, that was the hallmark of every Peerless Panthers basketball team: Playing with great heart, hustle, and determination. We were always the little guys, the underdogs, striving against all odds to overcome with tremendous grit and determination our physical limitations. That was Peerless basketball. That was the Panthers.

The reason I write about basketball with such emotion is that I didn't experience the game of basketball on a physical level. It wasn't about three-pointers, high fives and slam dunks. (Not that I could ever do that! Speaking of dreams!) I experienced basketball on an emotional, even a spiritual, level. I played basketball with my heart and so I write about it with my heart. My relationship with Jon, my relationship with Dad, with Ray, Bernie, Joel, and everyone you see in those pictures, is inextricably connected to the game of basketball.

Panther Support

In the locker room, despite my best efforts, I could not pull myself together. Leonard Hershel, a Panther supporter, told us "You guys don't suck no hind tit to nobody!" There were many, many other Peerless alumni consoling us in there as well. The unconditional support we had from the community was incredibly humbling. I remember hugging Bernie and him telling me how sad he was that this was the last game he would play with Jon and me. I also remember Willow Creek's point guard, Mark Korich, who was in the locker room as well, looking at me with concern, almost as if he couldn't comprehend what he was seeing. He said, "Hey, settle down, take it easy." I didn't even know him, had only just played against him the night before. But there was no way he could understand what I was feeling. It wasn't just about the State championship game. It was about my entire life.

To the Victors

In balloting done by sportswriters and sportscasters covering the tournament, Kevin Hatfield received 100 votes and Jon Puckett 97, it was the closest voting for MVP in several years. Had we won the championship, no doubt Jon would have won MVP again. Rounding out the first team All-State tourney were Skip Parker of Willow Creek, Ted Morefield of Roberts and Joe Puckett.

Joel Dighans headed up the second team, which included David Weltikol and Russell Edwards of Flaxville, Jeff Keller of Custer and Joe Neislanik of St. Regis.

At the time, Flaxville was only the third school in history to win State championships in its first two appearances at State. Superior did it in 1959 and 1963 (the only two times the team made it to State C), and Belfry did it in 1952, 53 and 54.

Final box score for State championship game:

> Flaxville: David Weltikol 16, Kevin Hatfield 24, Rocky Nelson 10, Mike Safty 4, Russell Edwards 8, Donny Cole 2, Jesse Cook 2

> Peerless: Jon Puckett 20, Joe Puckett 14, Joel Dighans 8, Ray Chapman 7, Bernie Wasser 1

No. 1 District in Class C

Here is an article about the dominance of District 1-C back then. It was written by Roy Pace of the Helena Independent Record following the State tourney:

"No. 1 district in Class C" by Roy Pace, Helena IR, March 13, 1979

> *The more than 100 Class C schools in Montana are divided up into 13 districts for basketball. And in the ranching and wheat farming area of extreme northeastern Montana the No. 1 means more than the number of the district.*

> *District 1-C, currently comprised of Antelope, Flaxville, Medicine Lake, Outlook, Peerless and Westby, has produced the Class C state champion four of the last five years. And twice during that time both teams in the state championship game came out of 1-C. Furthermore, Medicine Lake was the Class B state champion in 1975 before dropping back down to Class C.*

> *That corner of the state also produced the Class B state champion (Scobey) and runner-up (Plentywood) this year. Plentywood won the Class B title in 1978 and the Class A title in 1976. In 1975, that small area had three state champions, Poplar in A, Medicine Lake in B and Westby in C. And one school administrator attending the Class C Tournament over the weekend also pointed out that Billings West was AA champion that year, "and that is as close as you can get in AA,", meaning all of the power was in the East.*

> *A visit with a couple of school officials from northeastern Montana Saturday during the tournament reveals that competitive basketball begins in the third grade in many of the little schools. Also, Peerless and Flaxville (and probably*

several other schools) permit the students in the gym to play basketball about anytime they want to use the facility, summer or winter. All the boy or girl has to do is call up certain people in town and they will go down and let them in the gym to shoot around or play pickup games, or whatever they desire.

And as George "Tiny" Puckett, a member of the Peerless school board said earlier, "That is what we built the gym for. As long as they take care of it they can use it."

After I read this article, I thought it was kind of odd that people would think it noteworthy that we could get into the gym anytime we wanted. Guess I sort of took that for granted, because I didn't know anything else!

East has the Touch

This next article is my favorite article ever written about the 1979 Panthers, District 1-C and the State tournament in Helena. It was written by Daryl Gadbow, a sportswriter for the Missoulian, following the State 1979 tourney.

"West offers much but East has the touch," by Daryl Gadbow, Missoulian, March 1979

Think of it this way: western Montana has beautiful mountain scenery, sparkling rivers, boating, skiing . . .

What has eastern Montana got—besides high school basketball supremacy?

First, it was Scobey, destroying all opposition in the State Class B tournament two weekends ago. Saturday night a couple of Scobey's close neighbors in the extreme northeast corner of the state, Peerless and Flaxville, met for the Class C title in Helena.

At the same time Saturday, Lewistown was upending Glendive for the Class A crown, giving the east a clean sweep of prep champions and runners-up, for Montana's three smallest classification schools.

In Helena this past weekend, it was rumored that basketball is virtually a year-round occupation for youngsters in prairie towns such as Peerless. What else is there to do?

After the chores are finished in the summer, it's into the high school gym to sharpen those deadly shooting eyes and hone ball handling skills to a second-nature sharpness in pickup games.

Very few of the eastern Montana Class C schools participate in football. So, in the fall, after school, it's into the gym, where the boys practice against the girl's teams.

And they say Peerless' athletes run fast-break drills in the spring to prepare for track season.

All in all, it's a rather dreary existence when you think about it. In western Montana, there are just so many other things for people to do.

Peerless was a joy to watch, however, at the C tourney—a blur of five miniature, high-speed basketball automatons with radar shooting touches. The precision play of the Panthers' indistinguishable Puckett twins, Jon and Joe, enhanced the refined, almost mechanical image of the team.

The image dissolved immediately at the final buzzer of the championship game, as the Puckett twins simultaneously broke into tears at the reality of Flaxville's 66–50 victory sank in.

The contrast of both players and styles of play represented by the eight teams in the tourney was exemplified by that championship match-up. Flaxville was an extraordinarily tall team by Class C standards, led by 6–7 center Kevin Hatfield. The Cardinals' deliberate play was punctuated by devastating raw frontline power—the antithesis of Peerless' free-flowing style.

As you might suspect by now, my allegiances were with the smaller Panthers in the championship game, although they were by no means the underdogs, having beaten Flaxville three times during the season.

Like most of the fans at the tourney, I had to switch allegiances from the team I was originally most concerned with—the St. Regis Tigers, who were eliminated by Willow Creek Saturday morning.

Gaining a state tourney berth is often a rare occurrence for any particular team of the 97 Class C schools in Montana. It was, for example, the first trip to state in the school's history for St. Regis. As a result, qualifying for state becomes a major social event and an honor for the entire community.

So, to the Tigers' entourage (the lion's share of the population of St. Regis), add fans of three other feline species (including two varieties of Panthers), and the following throngs of three other assorted types of wild creatures (Broncs, Bears and Cardinals), plus the supporters of the Rockets (Rockets?) of Roberts, and eight flocks of brightly colored cheerleaders—and you have the makings of a Class C state tournament. And a riot.

The combined tensions of all those fierce local loyalties added up to a madhouse capacity—4,200 rabid spectators for each of the six tourney sessions during the three-day event at the Carroll College Physical Education Center.

Just try getting a last minute hotel or motel reservation in Helena during the tourney, or finding an empty seat in a restaurant between sessions, or (hah hah!) a ticket to the games once the tourney gets underway. No way.

An unpredicted snowstorm precipitated a snowball fight, with full-scale guerilla warfare tactics, among the tournament rivals in downtown Helena late Friday night after the semi-final games. The various "team color" windbreakers of the combatants sifted in and out of alleys and between parked cars as the forces gathered. Their fusillade of snowballs created a crisscrossing pattern under the streetlights.

No telling what kind of battles were waged in some of the motels. Surprisingly, Helena has survived this annual craziness for 25 years.

Since the tourney isn't over until after the championship game, (and there's no hollering whoa in the middle of a horse race), delegations of fans from the losing teams inevitably shifted their loyalty to one of the surviving teams.

The St. Regis bunch cast its lot with Flaxville.

It will long be remembered in St. Regis that the Tigers forced the 1979 state champions into overtime in the state tournament. And the Tigers have the mountains, too.

We are Gonna Beat You All

However, while our basketball team took second at State in 1979, the Peerless cheerleaders won first place, beating Flaxville, who also had a fantastic cheerleading squad. Our fabulous cheerleaders that year were Darla Drummond, Ronda Sletten, Barbie Trang and Judy Fouhy. Flaxville's cheerleaders were Melody French, Audrey Tryan, Teri Bjerke and Yvonne Legare.

Earlier that season, two of our cheerleaders, Judy Fouhy and Barbie Trang, wrote a custom-made cheer for our team, and part of it went like this:

"We are the Panthers,
And we're short and small,
And we are gonna beat you all!"

We almost did beat them all. All but one. All except, as it turns out, the team with the players that were, well, tall.

Epilogue

A Tale of Two Seasons

It is hard to resist comparing the two separate, but related, experiences of playing at State in 1978 and in 1979. If you want to have a bi-polar, schizophrenic experience in basketball this would be it. Talk about two extremes of experience! In 1978, we beat Flaxville, our archrival, in the challenge game at Wolf Point, coming from behind by eight points in the fourth quarter and ending a seven-game losing streak against them, to earn Peerless' first trip ever to State. Then, when we got to State, we were not expected to win a game; nobody knew who we were (except Outlook, of course), but then we caught the crowd and the tournament by surprise, and became the darlings of the tournament. We won three games, and ended the season on a spectacular last-second shot by Jon, beating Wibaux in the consolation. Jon was named MVP, and the fairytale season was complete. Not only that, Jon and I had still had our senior season in front of us! We weren't done! What a feeling!

Then, in 1979, we set the goal of winning the State tourney. We got to State, rolled through to the championship game, led by six mid-way through the third quarter, and then it was almost like someone said, "Let's see how we could script this ending so that it would the most terrible, unbelievably horrific, exact-opposite experience of the year before." And that is exactly what happened. Our archrival came from behind to beat us, shocked us, and in the end, Jon and I ended up playing on the court against Flaxville's subs on the grandest stage ever in Class C basketball, the Carroll College PE Center, the same stage on which we had seen played multiple State championship games in years past. Then, Kevin Hatfield edged out Jon for MVP, completing the perfectly symmetrical non-fairytale ending to the 1979 season.

The Recurring Dream

To this day, Jon and I have a recurring dream about playing at State, although I don't have this dream nearly as often as I used to. We discovered we shared the dream years later when I told Jon about it, and he told me he had the same dream! Here is how it goes . . .

It's January, after Christmastime. We're in our freshman year at college, and the District 1-C basketball tournament is coming up. Suddenly, I'm back from college, back home in Peerless in my bedroom. I'm going to school Peerless High. Except I'm not really attending classes, I'm just showing up at school so it looks like I'm a student again. Now I'm practicing with the Panthers in preparation for the District tournament. But I keep having this haunting thought; I think "This isn't legal. Jon and I are too old. Someone is going to discover that we're not eligible to play, that we've already graduated, and they're going to blow the whistle on us. None of this will count." But it is so much fun to play with the Panthers again. I'm so excited to have another opportunity to maybe play at State, and win it, that I just keep playing, hoping nobody will find out. We get to play through the District and Divisional tournaments, and we make it back to State. No one has blown the whistle on us yet, but I still feel guilty that this isn't really right.

Then, we're playing at State; we're kicking butt again, except I keep having that same haunting thought, that someone watching out there knows that this isn't legal. But we keep playing anyway because it's so much fun and we're winning, all the way to the State championship game. At times during the dream, I forget that it's not legit; I play on the court with Jon and the Panthers, and it's pure bliss. But then the thought comes back into my mind, that we're too old and are not eligible to play. I feel awful that we could end up winning the State championship this way, and that someone, even after that point, would call us out and it wouldn't count. Then, before the end of the State championship game, which we are winning easily, playing as well as we used to play when we were clicking, I look out at the crowd and know that they know that this isn't real, that it's not going to count. And then I wake up from the dream, before the game ends.

The Greatest Honor

At our athletic banquet later that spring, the announcement was made to retire Jon's and my numbers. This announcement came at the very end of the banquet, after all of the awards had been handed out, and it caught me completely off guard; I totally did not expect it, and it just overwhelmed me. It was John Hebnes who made the announcement. He called Jon and me up in front of the audience and said he had a "special announcement" to make. He was saying some very nice things about Jon and me, and then, at the end of his speech, he said that the decision had been made to retire our jerseys. The entire audience in the Peerless gym stood up and gave Jon and me a standing ovation. I'm not even going to try to describe what I was feeling at that point. I was so thankful that this was the last item on the agenda for the banquet. I literally had to run out of the gym and through the back door by the storage room in order to avoid everyone. It was all too much. All I could do was run home.

I have to tell all of you that this is such a tremendous honor, the most honorable award I've ever received, and ever will receive. In this book, I have revealed the reverence I had for Peerless basketball. I know that, like me, all the other players that ever wore a Panther uniform also played with enormous dedication, passion and intensity. That's what made the honor in some ways difficult to accept, because in my mind, all of us were deserving, not just Jon and me. All Jon and I ever did was to play the game we loved; we practiced hard to become the best players we could be. And all of the other Panther players did that too.

The success we enjoyed was due to a number of things: It took great leadership, for which I credit Marvin Hash; it took great coaching, which we had in Ron Scott, Clark Shaffer and Jim Niccum; it took Peerless teams that were successful before us, like the 1974 team, led by Don Puckett and Dallas Trangsrud, the first Peerless team to ever make it to Divisionals, and the 1975 team, who upset #1 Westby in the District semi-finals; it took the new gym, which gave us the opportunity to practice and prepared us to play on the court that we would play on during the tournaments; it took the entire Peerless community, the pep club and our cheerleaders supporting us like they always did, win or lose, in good times and bad, as we saw so clearly following the State championship game; it took our teammates, who were also dedicated and gave everything they had—especially role players (like Ross Chapman in 1977, Bill Fladager in 1978 and Ray Chapman in 1979), who are as necessary to a winning team as are the star players who get all the attention and headlines. Last and not least, it took my mom and dad, Tiny and Faustine Puckett, the two greatest parents a kid could ever have, totally dedicated to supporting and nurturing the love Jon and I had for the game of basketball, always there for us, encouraging us, win or lose, and providing us the very best possible opportunity to realize our lifelong dream of playing in and winning the State Class C tournament.

I never had a chance to say thank you to the entire Peerless community for that award. So now, thirty years later, all I can say is a very humble "Thank You." I have never felt more humble than when I would walk by the trophy case in the hallway of Peerless High School and see our numbers in there. No one has ever received an award that means more to them than what that award has meant to me, and I share it with all of you who have ever worn the Panther uniform, as well as with the entire Peerless community, with my mom and dad, and, most of all, with my brother Jon. Thank you for recognizing what Peerless basketball meant to us. I will never, ever forget it. And to think that what Jon and I and the rest of the 1978–79 Panthers accomplished might have inspired future Panthers to become better players and strive for greatness is, again, humbling.

Joni Jo

Following the 1978–79, season Coach Niccum left Peerless for another coaching job, and I never saw him after that. Also following the season, Coach Niccum's wife gave birth to a baby girl. Can you imagine our surprise when the Niccum's baby announcement card came to the Puckett house, and we opened the card to see the name of the baby girl? They'd named her, Joni Jo, in honor of Jon and Joe Puckett and the 1978–79 Panther season. In the card, Coach Niccum wrote a nice note telling Jon and me what an honor it was to coach us, and that that is why he named his girl Joni Jo. Coach Niccum, it was an honor to play for you. Thank you.

More Dancing

Following our two appearances at State in 1978 and 1979, Peerless teams in 1982, 1988 and 1995 made it back to the State tournament. In 1982, I watched the Peerless team, led by Wally Hames and Dwane Dighans, and coached by Bucky Henderson, play at the State tournament at Eastern Montana College in Billings. This Peerless team had also earned the right to play at State (as we had in 1978) by winning a challenge game at Divisional. This was an excellent team, the 1982 Panthers, and it was a very special experience to watch them play at State along with the rest of the Peerless fans. I knew them all, and they represented the fine tradition of Peerless basketball at State.

Then, in 1988, the Panthers, led by Jeff "Billy Balls" Jones and John Ray "Joe" Richardson, returned to the State tournament, again by winning a challenge game at Divisional. They were coached by Dave Selvig and Bernie Wasser. This team had to play short-handed at State because of injuries to two of their key players, Scott Fladager and Aaron Poser. Most Class C teams do not have a lot of depth; there simply are not a lot of players to choose from. Because of this, it was extremely difficult for the '88 Panthers to compete at State. I was not able to make this tournament. Having ruptured my Achilles tendon (playing basketball!) in January, I was in a cast that extended

The dream comes true in 1988 for Shawn Kegal, Jeff Jones and John Ray Richardson, as Peerless remains undefeated in Divisional challenge games. Photo by Melissa Kjos.

over my knee, and so I couldn't drive from Utah to Montana to see the games. They played at the Billings Metra in Billings.

Then, the last team to make it to State made up of players strictly from Peerless (later Peerless boys would make it to State as Scobey-Peerless co-op) were the 1995 Panthers, led by Jerod and Joel Nieskens, and coached by Paul Wick and Gary Nieskens. This team was very young, and they made an incredible tournament run, winning the Eastern divisional for the first time in our school's history. They then went on to take second at State. My dad and my brother Jon were there, and it was quite a thrill to watch this young Panther team accomplish what they did, to see them compete for the State championship game as we had done 16 years earlier. Jerod and

Joel reminded me of Jon and me, the way they played so well together. And their team reminded me of the 1978 Panthers; they surprised a lot of people in the tournament by making it as far as they did. They upset a very good Chester team in the semi-finals and then lost to an incredibly talented Belt team for the championship game. I also saw a lot of my other teammates there, like Willard and Bill Fladager, and the players from the 1982 and 1988 teams, as well as Peerless alumni from many different places.

A Common Thread

What was interesting to learn, as I dialogued with these players on the Peerless People group on Facebook, was that they shared our same dream, that of playing in the State C tournament. I also learned that the 1982 and 1988 teams really looked up to our 1978 and 1979 teams. They wanted to achieve, even surpass, what we had done. I was in the locker room after the 1982 Divisional championship game when Peerless lost to Outlook by a point. Jamey Snare was crying. He said, "We wanted to do what no Peerless team had done before." It was incredibly rewarding to discover that these later Peerless teams really looked up to us, and that they were playing with a sense of tradition for the Peerless Panthers basketball team, a team that now had a very fine tradition indeed.

Another thing I learned while discussing basketball with these former Panthers was that each player had an incredible amount of pride in *his* team and possessed a very loyal, unbreakable bond with *his* teammates. They had all grown up playing competitive basketball together since third grade, just as we had, and had shared the same experience. We started to discuss the "best" Panther team in history, the "best" Panther player in history, etc., and it was amazing to see how each team would select one of their own as the best in each category! "I'll take my teammates and lace 'em up against anybody, anytime," comments like that. Then, the conversation morphed into an Intra-Panther basketball tournament as we tried to determine the best team in Peerless Panther basketball history. So now, an alumni tournament, with the teams from 1978–79, 1982, 1988 and 1995, along with other Peerless teams, is being planned for June 2010. Of course, we will never know which was the best team in Peerless basketball history, or the best player, and that is as it should be. The Peerless Panthers were a fine basketball tradition, and all of us who ever wore the uniform were a part of it, and that is all we ever need to know.

One More Time

My last memory of the Peerless Panther basketball tradition stems from the Panther pep rally on Saturday afternoon, just prior to the Peerless vs. Belt State championship game at Brick Breeden Field-house in Bozeman, in March 1995. The concept (a great concept) was to have speeches delivered by players from Peerless teams that had previously been to State, the teams from 1978–79, 1982 and 1988. I remember Jamey Snare was there from the 1982 team and Jeff Jones from the 1988 team. The Peerless community was there in force, everyone from Peerless that could be there was there. Dad was there. Jon was there.

I was completely overcome by emotion. I remember telling Donna Fladager, a little bit before I was going to speak, that "I was a little emotional." I could get a little emotional at times, but this was overwhelming. It was 16 years earlier that our team had played for the State championship against Flaxville in Helena, and Peerless' appearance in the State championship game brought the emotions of that game back to me in a flood.

Growing up in Peerless, basketball for Dad, Jon and me was not just a game, it was our life, and this State C tournament and Panther team had brought the three of us, and the Peerless community, together one more time. When it was our turn to speak, Jon and I got up together, I had to grab onto Jon for strength; I couldn't get through it myself. His support helped, and I was able to start speaking. I remember looking out at the Peerless people in front of me. I remember seeing the face of Duke Trangsrud, and thinking about that amazing game in 1975 when his team upset Westby at District. I thought about the 1974 team led by Don Puckett and

Dallas Trangsrud that made it to Divisional for the first time in our school's history. I saw the parents of the kids. And I saw my dad, known to most people as "Tiny" Puckett.

The last time I saw my father before he died was at this State C basketball tournament. And isn't that appropriate? I left for Germany later that fall and was not able to make it back to the States to see him before he died, in the spring of 1998. This is my last image of him: he is looking at me as Jon and I speak to the Peerless community and the 1995 Panthers at the State C tournament. And I can see how proud of Jon and me he is and has been, and how proud of Peerless basketball.

Then I looked out at the team, the Panthers of 1995. I remember seeing their young faces. I remember seeing Joel Nieskens' face. He was sitting fairly close to me off to the left. He was looking up at me; I think he could sense the fire that was inside me, the passion I had at this moment, but I felt there was nothing I could really say to him or this team that could convey that. I couldn't put words to it. I remember telling them that no one had expected them to come this far, and that no matter what the outcome of the game was, as long as they played with heart and left everything out on the court, as we had done 16 years earlier, they would be champions. After I said that, everyone cheered really loudly, and I was kind of taken aback. I didn't expect it. And I told the team thanks for bringing us all together, my dad, Jon and me, former Peerless Panthers, and the Peerless community, one more time.

Now that I think about it, when Peerless Schools closed its doors forever in June 2009, there was not a State championship banner hanging in the gym, but it didn't matter; that's not what it was about. It was about all the fun we had playing basketball together growing up, the memories we still have of that time of our lives. And it was about how basketball was the one thing, the glue, the gravity, that brought us all together.

Notes on Photos

Page 3. My favorite memories of my dad and uncles together are of when I got to go on deer hunting trips with them in the fall when I was little boy. At the end of the hunting day, when we were in the camper together, the conversation would inevitably shift to basketball, and I just loved to listen to them discuss it.

Page 7. St. Ann's was located right across the street from Peerless High School. Often on a Sunday I would leave from church and go directly to the gym to play basketball. "Pray and Play!" I remember meeting Joel Dighans for the first time at Mass! Jon and I were baptized there by Father Kenney on March 31, 1961.

Page 10. The year 1937 was my dad's senior year in high school. They lost only three games all year and won the consolation at District (this photo), but didn't advance because the tournament was single elimination. The Pirates were next.

Page 12. The 1939 Peerless Pirates. Standing: Reese Puckett, George "Tiny" Puckett, Robert Hanson, Richard Halvorson, Ed Puckett. In front: Angelo Sparagno (my mom's brother, my uncle), Indy Halvorson and Dick Coram.

Page 16. I remember how excited I was the night this was put up. Marty Wasser was the foreman for the project. This particular winter the snow bank was so high I could almost dunk off it! Almost! Dad would often dreamily shoot around at this basket.

Page 18. Left to right: Jon Puckett, Murray Dighans, Matt Fouhy, Joe Puckett, Rick Wasser, Bernie Wasser, Ross Chapman, Bill Fladager, Ray Chapman. Team dog Snoopy is in front and Dad is in the back. Taken by Mom just across the street from our house.

Page 19. Standing left to right: Ross Chapman, Matt Fouhy, Jon Puckett, Rick Wasser, Joe Puckett, Bernie Wasser. Kneeling left to right: Brian Halverson, LeRoy Nelson, Dwane Dighans, Murray Dighans, Ray Chapman. Coach Tiny Puckett is standing in the back. In the old gym.

Page 20. Uncle Ed (left) had presented the fourth grade championship trophy to our team just moments earlier. His Hellcats girls team also played that night in front of a packed house in the old gym, the last school games played there.

Page 22. This was right after fifth grade championship game against Whitetail. We had just presented the "Goethe trophy" to Dad, seen in his left hand. Left to right: Rick Wasser, LeRoy Nelson, Bernie Wasser, Brian Halverson Matt Fouhy. Tiny went out a winner as a coach.

Page 24. Standing: Joe Puckett, Don Dorrie, Kelly Trang, Jon Puckett, Joel Dighans, Rick Wasser, Coach Ron Scott. Kneeling : LeRoy Nelson, Brian Halverson, Ray Chapman, Bernie Wasser, Matt Fouhy. We had just beat Antelope 59-29.

Page 25. Left to right: Bruce Dighans, Roger Trang, Jim Chapman, Andy Hershel, Tim Myers, Duke Trangsrud, Jack Snare, Tom Myers, Scott Dighans, Ross Chapman, Jody Snare, Steve Miner, Jim Myers. Lots of Panther smiles!

Page 32. Standing: Coach Shaffer, Willard Fladager, Kelly Trang, Rick Wasser, Joel Dighans, Marty Thieven, Bill Fladager, Coach Bechtold. Kneeling: Bernie Wasser, Roger Trang, Ray Chapman, Dwane Dighans, Jon Puckett, Perry Thieven, Joe Puckett.

Page 32. Left to right: Valarie Jones, Dannette Dighans, Darla Drummond, Barbie Trang and Judy Fouhy. Danette Pimperton and Kris Jones were mascots. Daniels County Leader photo.

Page 34. This was one of those games at Outlook where they blew us off the court early. Amazingly, in my high school career, we beat Outlook three out of four times on their home court, but not this game. That is Doug Selvig to the left, a sophomore at the time, Joe Puckett shooting and Les Sebastian to the right.

Page 44. This was very late in the third quarter. For Outlook: Jerry West, Les Sebastian, Doug Selvig and Kevin Ordahl. For Peerless: Roger Trang, Joe Puckett and Bill Fladager.

Page 47. Left to right for Flaxville: Cory Tryan, Kevin Hatfield, Jesse Cook. Left to right for Peerless: Joe Puckett, Joel Dighans, Bill Fladager, Jon Puckett, Roger Trang. Part of Westby's "We Have Ranger Pride" banner can be seen to the right. This banner was snipped in two following Peerless' upset of #1 Westby at District in '75.

Page 50. Rolly Starkey, seen here defending Joel Dighans, was an excellent center for Richey. He was first team All-State that year. Although Joel Dighans defended him well in this game, he still scored 24 points against us. We stayed in our 2-1-2 zone the entire game, but constantly pressured their guards out front to force turnovers.

Page 52. Left to right for Outlook: Randy Wangerin and Les Sebastian. Left to right for Peerless: Bill Fladager, Joel Dighans, Joe Puckett and Roger Trang. I really hadn't had time enough to think that if we won this game we would go to State. We almost came back to win this one late, but had to wait till Monday for a ticket to State.

Page 64. This photo was taken in the first half, when the pace of the game was very slow and the game was being played in the half court.. Kevin Hatfield played extremely well in the loss for Flaxville this game, scoring 20 points. In the photo for Peerless are Jon and Joe Puckett and Joel Dighans. Wolf Point Herald-News photo.

Page 66. Bernie shot this free throw while we were leading late in the game. For Flaxville: David Weltikol, Kevin Hatfield, Jesse Cook and Wade Tryan. For Peerless: Bill, Joel and Bernie. Not shown are Joe and Jon Puckett at half court, smiling at each other and shaking their heads in disbelief.

Page 68. Roger Trang and Bill Fladager accept second place trophy for Peerless. Karl Fiske of Medicine Lake, a Montana High School Association (MHSA) officer, made the presentation. Tedi Hash can be seen clapping in the background to the right of Roger. Daniels County Leader photo.

Page 69. Left to right: Bill Fladager, Rick Wasser, Joe and Jon Puckett, Coach Shaffer, Perry and Marty Thieven. This was a rough ride for Coach. Not something we practiced every day! W.P. Herald-News photo.

Page 70. This is one of the beautiful things about being the first to do something. We had just finished second in the tourney, but we were champions, headed to State for the first time in our schools' history. I heard someone in the crowd say, "Hey, you don't take the nets when you take second." Do you think I cared?

Page 81. This was in the first half, before we really started to get out and run. The shot looks straight and true doesn't it? Unfortunately, Richard Begger of Wibaux (left) got a piece of this ball, and it barely made it to the basket! Wibaux was in their extended 1-3-1 zone at this point of the game. Photo by Helena IR Bill Bowman.

Page 85. Manhattan Christian had an outstanding front line that year. Two of them are shown here, center Randy Van Dyk (left) and forward Lee Logterman (right). Christian's frontline of Van Dyk, Logterman and Lee Kimm had 61 points and 42 rebounds against us that night. Photo by Independent Record's Bill Bowman.

Page 89. This photo captures what a tremendous rebounder Joel Dighans was. Lin Soholt of Brady, 6'3", is fighting Joel for the ball. Panthers in the photo are (from left) Jon and Joe Puckett and Bill Fladager. Pictured for Brady are Kirby Kauk, Soholt and Kevin Kauk, Brady's All-State guard. Photo by Helena IR Bill Bowman.

Page 92. Joel Dighans jumps against Wibaux's Todd Leach. Leach, , a superb athlete, was selected first team All-State team that year (for the season) and he was second team All-State tourney, as was Joel. Pictured for Peerless are Bill Fladager and Roger Trang. In the background to the right is the Peerless crowd at State.

Page 96. Panthers leave the court just after their thrilling last second consolation game win over Wibaux in '78. Pictured for Peerless are Ray Chapman (10) Roger Trang (24) and Bill Fladager (32), who is getting a hug from his dad Lalon.

Page 97. The roar from the crowd was deafening when Roger and Bill walked out to receive the trophy. The "Powers in the East" chant started up, and I remember hearing a fan from Manhattan Christian sitting near me say, "But Christian's in the West!". It was surreal watching this. So many people cheering for Peerless!

Page 98. Dave Selvig, Randy Wangerin and Jerry West from Outlook receive first place trophy, State '78. In all the years I played basketball, I never saw three guys play better together than these three. They knew each so well on the court it was almost as if they moved as one player. Absolutely brilliant.

Page 106. This photo of Jon by Bill Bowman of the Independent Record appeared with the Associated Press article announcing that Jon Puckett had been named MVP at the State tournament. It was unusual for the third place team to have the MVP, although it had happened before in 1973 when Randy Selvig was named MVP after Outlook took third at State.

Page 110. Standing: Coach Brian Bechtold, Murray Dighans, John Machart, Mike Mattson, Rick Wasser, Joel Dighans, Matt Fouhy, Ray Chapman, Coach Jim Niccum. Kneeling: Mike Machart, Brian Halverson, Jon Puckett, Bernie Wasser, Joe Puckett, Dwane Dighans.

Page 110. Standing: Barbie Trang, Darla Drummond and Ronda Sletten. In front is Judy Fouhy. Our cheerleaders were selected as the best cheerleaders at the State tournament in 1979. "We are the Panthers and we're short and small . . ."

Page 113. This is me running at our home cross country meet in Sep '78, which we won. Our course was very difficult; it had the steepest hill on any course I'd ever run on. It could suck you dry! We would train for cross country for two hours after school, eat dinner, then play basketball at the gym for two hours at night. Pure bliss.

Page 115. This picture of Coach Niccum was taken at State in '79. It looks as if he is raising his fist in triumph; but, as Ray Chapman correctly recalls, he is calling for a play named "Fist". Cliff Hagfeldt, colorful (and funny!) radio announcer for KCGM "the voice of the prairies" in Scobey, always referred to Coach Niccum as "Diamond" Jim Niccum.

Page 130. Peerless and Bainville leaving the court after PCIT game, 1978. Players pictured on the left are (front to back) Bernie Wasser, John Machart and Rick Wasser; on the right are Ray Chapman, Jon Puckett, Joel Dighans and Mike Mattson.

Page 131. Peerless vs. Scobey, PCIT 1978. Scobey players left to right: Dan Danelson, Don Boos and Brad Henderson. Peerless players in man-to-man defense from left to right: Joel Dighans, Ray Chapman, Jon and Joe Puckett.

Page 132. Peerless vs. Scobey, PCIT 1978. Dan Danelson shoots against Peerless. Scobey players (from left) are Don Boos, Kelly Norman and Kirby Halvorson. Peerless players are Matt Fouhy, Bernie Wasser, Jon Puckett, Joel Dighans and Joe.

Page 134. Peerless vs. Flaxville at Peerless, '79. Cardinals in photo left to right: Kevin Hatfield, Russell Edwards, Mike Safty and Rocky Nelson. Panthers are Joel Dighans, Jon Puckett and Matt Fouhy. This was the first of five games between the two rivals.

Page 144. Ray Chapman shoots in warm ups prior to Westby game, kicking off the March to Helena in '79. Two very attentive Peerless fans, Tiny and Faustine Puckett, can be seen sitting to the left, ready to go!

Page 148. Flaxville and Peerless cheerleaders unveiled this banner prior to District championship '79. Flaxville cheerleaders in photo: Teri Bjerke, Audrey Tryan, Yvonne Legare, Melody French. Banner was red-white-blue-gold.

Page 149. We were trailing 15–11 toward the end of the first quarter. I knew at this point we had to take our game up another level if we were going to win this game. And we did just that!

Page 153. Jon Puckett takes the nets following District championship game against Flaxville. Taking the nets is not any easy thing to do if you've never done it before. It's not something we practiced. Scissors and ladders tend to help out a lot.

Page 154. Peerless Panther co-captains Ray Chapman, Jon and Joe Puckett receive the first place trophy at District '79. Somehow, Jon won the lottery and got to wear the net around his neck. Joel Dighans got the other one. I just clutched the trophy tightly.

Page 173. Rocky Nelson of Flaxville holds up the first place trophy at Divisional '79. Cardinals in picture are (from left) Conley Bjerke, Rocky Nelson, David Weltikol, Mike Safty and Kevin Hatfield. P-Herald photo.

Page 187. The inimitable Super Panther (SP). The masked super hero, Annabelle Fouhy, was brilliant in her role. The pep rallies we had were extremely creative and fun. Usually the script for an SP scene called for SP to put out a fire the boys couldn't quite squelch on their own. Appearances by SP were rare. Only at tournament time.

Page 189. My favorite picture of Mom and Dad. Dad soaked up the attention at State and was never shy at granting an interview. This photo, taken by Bill Bowman, was for an Independent Record article written by Roy Pace entitled "The Pucketts have been here before," which appeared on the day of State championship '79.

Page 190. Two MVPs at State. I am not sure if this has happened before or since the State C tourney in '79. Ross Chapman captured the essence of this picture by writing (on Facebook) "The picture symbolizes, in a nutshell, the different styles of play of the two teams. Run and gun vs. more of a half-court set." Photo by IR Bill Bowman.

Page 197. This photo by Bill Bowman was taken at the start of Willow Creek game. Dighans won the tip and I immediately attacked the basket on the dribble. Willow Creek players are Mark Korich, Skip Parker and Dana Williams. Skip Parker was voted first team All-State tourney, averaging 19 points and 14 rebounds a game.

Page 201. In this photo, taken in the first half, Jon is readying his feet to shoot a jump shot off the dribble after getting a screen from Ray Chapman. Rocky Nelson is defending for Flaxville. You can bet the open look Jon has at this point will be closed in quickly by a switch out from a Flaxville defender. Photo by IR Bill Bowman.

Page 202. We set more screens on the ball against Flaxville this game than we normally did. It was hard to get open looks off the ball. In this photo, Bernie Wasser is setting a screen on David Weltikol. This picture shows the double attention I was getting this game, as Russell Edwards normally guarded me. Photo by Bill Bowman.

Page 205. It is unbelievable to me that this picture was taken when it was, with Peerless leading 35-29 and 4:33 left in the third quarter. This is when Flaxville's 15-2 run began. Russell Edwards passed the ball into David Weltikol who was fouled. He made one free throw to begin the run to end the quarter. Photo by Bill Bowman.

Page 206. Again, amazing the timing of this photo. Weltikol opened the scoring in the fourth quarter with this basket. Jon had three fouls and had to avoid picking up his fourth. This is actually from a series of photos taken by Bill Bowman and it reveals the desperation that was beginning to show on the faces of the Panthers.

Page 209. This photo was taken by Dad just moments after we received the second place trophy. Coach Niccum is to the left, Ray Chapman is bent over in front. Jon is holding the trophy behind Ray. Joe Puckett and Joel Dighans are to the right of Ray.

Page 222. This photo captures the moment when the dream of making it to State comes true. In this case, for 1988 Panthers Shawn Kegal, Jeff Jones and John Ray Richardson. This photo was taken following their challenge game win over Saco. Photo by Melissa Kjos.

The Last Letter

This section contains the text of a letter I received from my cousin Terry Puckett, just before the school closed its doors for the final time in June 2009. Terry was the last Superintendent of Peerless Public Schools. The photos below the letter are of the bear he gave me with the blue and gold Panther letterman jacket.

Hi Joe,

I thought you might like the little bear with the Panther jacket as a memory from the school. It's what I gave the staff and kids our last day of school. Grandpa got the high school started in the fall of '32. The annexation to Scobey is effective July 1, 2009.

The school's memorabilia was donated to the Daniels County Museum: all the trophies, class pictures, plaques, your picture and jersey, etc. The school donated money to the museum for the use and future upkeep of the dedicated room. The room is small, 12'x19', so they will have to occasionally rotate donated items.

I hope everything is going great for you!

Terry Puckett

Peerless High School, 1932–2009

Index